The
Horse
Husband

The
Horse
Husband

WHEN NEIGH MEANS YES

Stan Nahman

Deeds Publishing | Atlanta

For Beverly, with love and a smile.

Introduction

Drawn into horses the fourth year of my marriage, I did not know it would shape my world for the next 30 years.

A glimpse of the future came at a horse party in 1989. Mingling, I joined a small group of horse husbands gathered in a safe place, away from the women. I lamented to the group over the long lives of horses. "At least with kids, there's a chance they will move out after a couple of decades. Horses last much longer, contributing nothing and consuming resources until they die." I paused at a sudden insight, "But at least when they do die, we go down by one."

One guy sipped his beer and shook his head. "That's not the end. They just buy another one." My optimism crushed, I realized I was in it for the long haul.

On my own, I turned to the keyboard and decided to log my experiences. At least when I die, and she goes down by one, I will have left a mark.

So in the end, this collection of horse stories, based on my experiences, with occasional literary hyperbole to keep it interesting, is written for men, by a man, and I expect will never be read by a man. In all likelihood only women, including your wife, will read this. Whether new to the game or a veteran, you might as well plan for the coming shift in your future.

She will look at you, her arm still in a sling from the minor surgery she required after getting kicked by the horse you have always hated, and with her good hand, point at my small book sitting on the coffee table. "Melvin, that horse husband guy says we have to get some Metamucil for the babies, stall mats for the barn's center aisle, and I don't care if you have to unload it, I'm ordering a semi of decent hay from Idaho next year."

Happy horsin', Melvin.

Stan Nahman
Aiken, SC

CHAPTER 1

The Eleventh Commandment

Hello, boys. Have you ever heard something like this from your horsewoman: "Do you think we should put root beer flavoring in Gideon's water?"

There is so much wrong with this question that it's hard to know where to start. We can begin with the fact that Gideon is a horse, not her demented uncle. We then move to other issues including why is she asking *your* opinion, what does she mean by *we*, and root beer flavor for a horse? *Can she be serious?*

A non-horse male will be so confused by the question that he will foolishly ask, "What are you talking about?" He will never get back the 30 minutes it took for her to answer.

The schooled equestrian male will offer a simple response, "If you think he will like it," knowing it is an absurd answer to a more ridiculous question. But it keeps the peace and brings closure to the issue. And there's always the longshot that root beer will make Gideon less obnoxious. I never thought glucosamine would make my knee feel better either.

If you are hanging with a horsewoman (henceforth referred to as a horse wife), then married or not, you are a horse husband. You do not call the shots when it comes to her horses, but that's okay. Since you remain a couple, she must still like you, in large measure because you recognize your profound shortcomings around horses. Two major limitations may include a negligible attention span, or your annoying tendency to jump to solutions rather than discussing, in painstaking detail, the problem. But you do bring something to the table — the provision of support; emotional, physical, and, if you are still working, financial. The latter is important, for she may also work. Hell, with horses, you *both* may *have* to work.

She may be the primary breadwinner. Don't let it bug you. She'll admit that your meager salary helps pay for horse feed. This places you one rung above manure, which is the fate of all horse feed. Oh well, better fate than never.

A general blueprint for a life well-lived may be found in the Ten Commandments. In addition to the Ten, your life with horses will be seamless if you add an Eleventh: "Thou shalt not seek thy woman's love when she is in the barn."

A classic violation of this iron-clad rule includes interrupting when she is grooming her horse.

One day, you make the mistake of walking out to the barn for a short discussion about golf. Dressed in a classic oxford shirt with a light blue university stripe, clean jeans, and soft Sketchers, you consider that you should have worn barn clothes. You shake off the foreboding sensation and enter the barn. After all, you're not here to work, you just need to have a quick conversation. Stepping around piles of horsehair, you approach a half-sleeping little gelding standing in the cross ties, while your demure wife seems to be giving a horse-backrub with a heavy wire loop. Dust swirls in the streaming sun-light, and you fear for your shirt.

A soft cough gets her attention. "The guys have a tee time tomorrow. Can I play?"

She tugs on a red hairball tangled in the curry comb, and speaks without looking up.

"I am going to ride after this. Since you are here, can you pick his hooves?"

She's referring to the business of picking grunge (consisting of manure and mud) out of the bottom of each foot, a task with which you are familiar. It requires squatting then cradling each hoof in one hand and, using a hoof pick that looks like a bent nail with a wooden handle, excavate chunks of brown stink from the bottom of the foot. Considering your attire, this is utterly unthinkable.

Staying strong, you counter. "I'm not dressed for barn work right now."

The comb clean, she pauses to give you the once-over. "Oh. Okay. What did you want?"

Under the full force of her attention, you mumble your request again. You get the green light for golf. The experience reminds you not to visit the barn for important matters. She will be focused on nothing but her horse, thus confirming The Commandment.

If this sounds familiar, your wife is representative of the entire horse wife species. I have never met your wife, but I know her. They are all the same. At a party, horse girls who are perfect strangers will soon be talking like they are long-lost sisters.

"Hi, I'm Shelly, we have the farm on Route Three."

"I'm Peggy, is yours the place with the gray warmblood? We pass it on the way to the show grounds."

"Yes, that's us! I think I've seen you at the show. Do you train with…" And, just like that, the bond is established.

By the end of the night they'll make plans to meet for lunch, attend a dressage clinic the following Saturday, and be sure to exchange cute little Christmas ornaments that look like horses.

Meanwhile, the men will keep it short, enduring the party until they can leave.

"Did you see the Falcons play Sunday?"

"Yeah, they sucked."

"I'm Jim."

"Stan."

Both will forget the names in moments, and neither will feel guilty about it.

The Eleventh Commandment may apply beyond the barn, including a meal.

You may be out for a nice dinner. She sips her wine and offers a thoughtful look. "Do you think Wally is happy?"

Wally is not the neighbor's dysfunctional teenage girl with a boy's name but is a fifteen-year-old gelding your wife bought in Florida four years ago. Twelve months later, he sustained a suspensory injury, becoming un-ridable. He has been hanging around your farm ever since, eating, producing manure, and shedding red hair every spring.

"Ah, well, I'm not sure." Since you have no idea what she is talking about, but feel reckless, you ask, "Why?"

Her concentration, unfettered by the half-consumed glass of Merlot, is total. "Something is off with him."

Uncertain what she means, you forge ahead. "How so?"

"He just doesn't look right."

The last time you thought a horse didn't look right was when Mongo from *Blazing Saddles* punched one out in the middle of the street.

The salads come and you are spared further comment. The second bottle of Merlot also helps, keeping the conversation in familiar territory—money, why you want a bigger television, and whether you are ever going to use the elliptical you bought last winter. The meal concludes with plans for her to go visit her sister, the horse forgotten for the moment.

The following week, Wally and the other three horses got de-wormed. A check of Wally's poop showed a writhing bundle of intestinal worms.

Her suspicions confirmed, she gives you that knowing look. "See? I knew there was something wrong. He looks happier already."

You do not comment that most people, and probably most animals, look happier after what Wally did.

As much as The Commandment is straightforward, there are gaps. Consider seeking her love *while in service to a horse* or *the horse mission*. It works. She will love you for simple tasks. Easy offerings include hand-grazing Wally for an hour, cleaning the spider webs out of the rafters of the barn, or suggesting the two of you go to a tack store so she can shop. The latter, far beyond the call of duty, should be reserved for big-ticket items, like asking about the golf trip with the guys to Lake Tahoe.

A hidden emotion lurking behind The Commandment is worry. She won't be interested in you seeking her love if she is concerned about a horse. You think she is still mad about the trailer hitch you bought for her fortieth birthday but odds are, she is upset about a horse-related matter.

There is not enough space here to list all the horse worries keeping your wife edgy during the day and awake all night, but a few include the price of feed, the quality of hay, gnats, and a vast and never-ending source of angst, lameness.

Every horse has four legs, with at least three joints and a hoof per leg that can cause lameness. That is sixteen possible lame-potential sites per horse. We have four horses, ballooning the total number to sixty-four. This helps explain why we always seem to have at least one horse hobbling around at any given time. She knows these numbers; she worries.

Riding in the arena one day, she called to me as I puttered with a broken sprinkler head.

"Does Fletcher look like he's off to you?"

To me, Fletcher looked like a horse with a rider. "Nope."

"His left hind is off. I can feel it at trot and canter. Watch." She kicks it up to trot then a gentle canter. Once again, you see nothing but a horse with a rider, but going faster. "See?"

"Ah, not really."

"He's off."

She dismounts, takes a now happier Fletcher into the barn, removes the bridle, slips him into a halter and hands the shank to you before pulling the remaining tack.

"Put him in the cross ties and give him a few of these treats."

The size of a Brussels sprout, the apple-flavored nuggets are an outrageous two dollars each. This is why we later switched to Honey Nut Cheerios from Costco—cheaper and gobbled with the same enthusiasm as the ridiculous pseudo apples.

As you feed Fletcher money, she does a detailed assessment of the left hind leg, revealing nothing.

Over the next two days, his gaits worsen to the point where even you can see he is off. She does not sleep. Lake Tahoe feels like a pipe dream. On the third day, she picks up the left back foot and using a metal probe, pokes around the edge of the bottom of the hoof where she discovers a hoof abscess. With a dig and a scrape, it drains foul yuck. She cleans it with a betadine solution and within a day she reports the return of normal gaits.

Trying to seek anything from her when she is worried about a horse will lead to disappointment. In this case, we lost three days of happiness to a hoof abscess, but I was astute enough to not go seeking.

So boys, stay alert and remember the Eleventh Commandment. With a little foresight, you just might make it to Tahoe where you can brag about your "stable" marriage.

Happy horsin'.

CHAPTER 2

Fashion Statements

Hello, boys. Barn attire is of sufficient import for elaboration. Why would a horse husband write about this and why should you care? Because if you want to keep the horses and their smells out of your house, you must establish firm rules about clothing.

Our horse friend, Gabby from Ohio, gave my wife advice about the advantages of having your own farm. "You can go out and feed in your pajamas if you want to!"

Not at our house. Those pajamas will be the next set of barn clothes. They will smell, and not of humans, but of horse urine, manure, dust, and, depending on the season, fly spray. In fairness to Gabby, she has given us many useful suggestions, but this was not one of them.

The rule that says you cannot get closer than two hundred yards to a barn without getting dirty, is true. Dedicate some crummy clothes to the mission, hang them in your garage, and change whenever you need to go to the barn. Change every time. Every trip to the barn includes mixing with stink and getting dirt and dust on your clothes. Clothes also include shoes. No exceptions. Get muck boots or knee-high rubber boots and use them.

I learned about shoes the hard way. One day, during our first winter at the farm in Ohio, it was two degrees and everything was frozen. I had a great pair of leather hiking boots, comfortable and warm, so I wore them out to the barn for early morning chores. The cold day soon included snow, so I wore the boots to work. During the 27 mile commute, the car warmed up and it smelled like the barn again. It was not subtle. On reflection, I realized my knobby Vibram soles were clogged with noxious tidbits from the floor of the barn, unsmellable at two degrees, but brought back to life with warming. The foul organics had settled into the crevasses of the soles (not to be confused with horse wives where horses settle into the crevasses of *their* souls).

The closer I got to work, the stronger grew the smell. Helpless since the windows were frozen shut, I drove on, teary-eyed. At work and engulfed in horse-stall smog the entire day, people glared at me for stinking up a room. Unlike the rubber of a muck boot, the leather in my shoes hung on to the stink. That day was their last barn tour. Goodwill even rejected them.

Your horse wife has a different set of problems. She may need shoes for riding, showing, wearing out to dinner with the girls, driving the truck, or just hanging around the barn. Covering these activities can result in shoe-numbers in the hundreds. In fairness to all horsewomen, I have exaggerated. I took the liberty of estimating the total shoe count. Divide by two to get the number of pairs, it will seem smaller.

Like most women's footwear, horse-related shoes range

from ugly and comfortable (Crocs) to less ugly but uncomfortable (stilettos). Lacking personal experience, I depend on others regarding the comfort of stilettos. I cannot imagine why anyone would wear them to the barn. Although tight black riding pants combined with stilettos and a crop evokes a series of stereotypic images.

For your wife, there is a "barn casual" shoe for dinner with the girls, a semi-disco boot. Despite a nice sweater or top (with horse logo somewhere), jeans, and a leather belt with turquoise inlaid into a silver buckle, the ensemble is destroyed by the shoes. Remember those black boots the Beatles wore in the sixties? No? Take a look at Ringo on the cover of Abbey Road. No matter, that ridiculous Beatle boot with or without a zipper on the inside part of the upper, is the casual shoe for trips away from the barn. I did not like them on Ringo and they are no better on a horse girl. The terrible look is magnified if worn with riding pants. Tight at the ankle, the pants leave the entire tacky boot exposed. Jeans at least offer a small chance for coverage. You probably know what I am talking about and have likewise discovered that your opinion in this area is irrelevant.

The other crazy shoes of your wife's world are riding boots. They are skintight to the knee and always too small for the foot. Once on, never off. I have seen my poor wife work up a bigger sweat putting the damn things on than she does riding her horse. But getting into the shoe is only half the job. Once done riding, she has to remove them. Using a plus-size boot jack and 2,000 calories, she grunts and groans as she extracts her feet from a quicksand grip. But if the ride was good, she didn't remember the boots.

Less a fashion statement than a necessity, are helmets. The internet is flush with terrible stories of young, helmetless riders who have suffered heinous neurologic injuries from falls. The dressage governing bodies now allow helmets in lieu of a top hat. So, helmets are good. On the other hand, they are horse helmets, not bike helmets. To a horse wife, there is no difference, except a horse helmet is better. We explored this issue with a bike ride.

She handed me a horse helmet known to fit my big head. "Here, use this one. It will give better protection than that white plastic thing you have worn since the eighties."

I shrugged. "Fine by me."

She had gone to a lot of trouble to find me a good horse helmet. It was comfortable but not necessary since I had stopped riding. The reasons exceed the word count of this essay, so I will leave it for later. But, I was familiar with the helmet and was happy enough to wear it.

The bike ride was an easy four miles out, stop for lunch, and four miles back.

As we pedaled along, she looked at me in my helmet and smiled. "It looks good on you."

I stole a glance. "It feels pretty good, but I am getting a cramp in my neck."

"You are just hungry."

By the end of the fourth mile, I knew why the horse helmet protected better, it weighed three times my little Styrofoam job from the eighties. The pressure from the weight was exaggerated by the posture common to most bike riders; full extension of the neck while leaning over the handlebars with your back flexed like the "cat" move in yoga. Without neck extension, you can't see the road, raising the likelihood that the helmet may become necessary.

By lunch, I had a splitting headache and a knotted neck. I wanted a Motrin more than a sandwich. I rode back helmet-less, my neck de-torking and my wife on full alert for potential accidents. No more horse helmets on the bike. Besides, in the single wreck I had on my bike, the crummy thing from the eighties did just fine, in fact, since I hit a parked truck, the helmet and I did better than the bike, which had to be replaced.

I will close the clothes with coats. Barn coats. I have two for when a coat is needed; a beat-up semi-water resistant parka shell and a gauche ski jacket, both over 30 years old. It's Aiken, so the need for coats is rare, but when necessary, these two get me through fall and winter. Since I have been influenced by my wife's interest in coats, I accept the fact that I may have twice what I need, and to other horse husbands, appear extravagant. I don't care what you think, you are not my boss.

Horsewomen may have many coats. In my experience, I have concluded they may need a coat for riding, showing, out with the girls, mucking, holding the shank for the farrier, meeting the equine dentist, or driving the tractor for spreading manure or dragging the arena. I can count at least eight potential "coat-able" activities for each of two seasons (cool and cold), approximating 16 necessary coats. Then there is two-season rain which may affect at least three of the above, bringing the total coat count to an even 22. Not that the above is our situation, but I use it as an example.

I think part of the spike in coats is also related to the internet. My wife scours the cyber world for good deals. Amazon has our Visa number, so coats can proliferate with a simple click. Since her targets are always on sale and horse-related, Equinomics applies (see Chapter 3) and we never lose money.

So, if the above is not "Say yes to the dress," neither does it "Say no to the show." Fashion has its place in the barn and on the farm. Your wife knows the formula, do what she says, but help keep it real. Your job is to temper her desires for more stuff, as well as her assertive plan to wear her PJs to the barn. If bringing this up is risky, just wear your horse helmet to the discussion. She'll laugh at you, but it will at least soften her to your point of view.

Happy horsin'.

CHAPTER 3

Equinomics Is The New Math

Hello, boys. Today's horse husband lesson deals with the dollars you think you are losing on horses. You can relax. Not only have you not lost money, but your net worth has also increased. This is the beauty of Equinomics.

Equinomics, a portmanteau of the words "equestrian" and "economics," refers to the finances and curious cash flow associated with horses. Like chaos theory, Escher drawings, and quantum mechanics, it can be difficult to grasp at first. Simply put, the bottom line is *never* in the red. Never. At worst, we always break even, Horses *never* cost you money.

Horse husbands must learn the basics of Equinomics if they are to maintain sanity. This includes understanding some of the necessary costs. A few general rules: 1) Do not ask why you have 12 halters for three horses, 2) Don't bug her about the horse insurance she just bought. Everybody does that once, then realizes it's not worth it. She won't do it again, and 3) Remember, pre-sale vetting helps everybody but the guy selling the horse (which is you). It is a clever way for vets to make money while they equivocate on a diagnosis, and for the buyer, the ambiguity of the evaluation always allows for a cut in the offer. My advice is to take the offer anyway and get rid of the horse.

This nugget of wisdom came from my friend, Ollie from Ohio, who dropped out of law school to do horses fulltime. He is my horse guru and among the few who make money in the business.

Years ago, he spoke of selling horses. "Stan, if ya get an offer, just take it."

I thought, *no way, we'll negotiate*. "Why's that?"

With the seasoned gaze of a thousand horse sales, Ollie explained, "If you want ten grand, and they offer eight, what's your response?"

My wife would be offended at such a gauche offer for her horse, but I kept this to myself. "Stinks, it's a low ball offer."

"Yep and your wife will be so pissed the buyer doesn't see the value of her horse, she won't even bother to counter."

See, he's a guru. "Yep."

He raised his eyebrows. "So she refuses the offer, knowing a smarter buyer will come along. But it takes a year."

Unsure of the direction of the conversation, I squinted but agreed. "No doubt."

He offered a wry smile. "So, over the next year, you spend $100 a month for grain and hay, $500 for shoes and toe trimming, $200 in random vet bills, and another $1,000 in lessons. That's $2,900. Never mind ancillary costs on horse chiropractors, acupuncturists, and psychics. Add another $500 for that and you've spent $3,400."

I nod. "By waiting a year, we've incurred costs over the

original offer of eight grand, exceeding the original $10,000 asking price by $1,400."

"Yep, sell the horse. Each year, it's costing you money. In this case, waiting would cost you $3,400."

I reported this depressing news to my wife, who was quick to point out the problem with Ollie's logic. "It looks like we are down $3,400, but we aren't. We still have the horse. We would have spent the money anyway for a net gain of $3,400. The training has made a huge difference, so now we can ask $15,000 instead of ten, for an additional gain of $5,000. See, we are already up $8,400. And remember, we only paid $9,000 for the horse three years ago, so if we get $15,000, that is another six grand, putting us ahead by $14,400."

This ridiculous logic explains why I will work fulltime until I'm 90.

If this bamboozles you, perhaps an illustrative case will clarify the stunning power of Equinomics.

A horse husband from Ohio named Bob, and his horse wife Jennie, bought a horse named Velcro for $12,000. Velcro was 11, a good mover, and trained to the third of eight levels of dressage. A novice rider, Jennie lacked the skills necessary to ride the horse. She hired Sarah, a trainer, and made progress. Winter came to Ohio, making horse training a chilly and sparse business; so Sarah followed the weather and the money to Florida.

Sarah told Jennie, "Velcro could be worth some money, so why not send him to West Palm with me? I can put in the needed training."

Jennie agreed. Bob was on board since it meant one less

horse to feed during his morning rounds. Two months into training (at $1,500 per month), Velcro was making progress toward advanced levels of dressage. Sarah called, reporting that she could get 40 grand for him today and 60 with another month of training.

Bob was thrilled with the 40, telling Jennie, "Sell the horse."

He cared little about the money, but the prospect of being down one horse was very attractive. He laughed as he told me the story. "The whole idea of being *paid* to be down one horse was ridiculous. Hell, I would have been happy to pay somebody to *take* the horse."

Jennie wanted to give Sarah a chance with one more month of training and see where they'd be. Since he had zero input anyway, Bob agreed.

"We should have sold," he told me.

One week after Jennie agreed to the additional month of training, a late-night call came from Sarah. It looked like Velcro was having a severe episode of colic. The vet recommended urgent surgery. Jennie was conflicted, but Bob knew it was a no-brainer. Velcro would get his surgery. Five minutes later, Jennie approved the operation. The vet required a Visa card number to operate; it was given and under the knife went Velcro.

The next morning, Velcro was doing well; his bowels were fine and the surgeon found no other internal abnormalities.

Bob squinted at me. "I wondered if the vet was more about business than vetting."

Bob went to work that day, and on the way home, he stopped for gas. For some inexplicable reason, the gas pump would not take his credit card, causing angst, and forcing a cash transaction.

When he got home, Jennie gave him the favorable report on Velcro: his first day went well.

Bob retired to his office to call the credit card company.

"This is how we found out what it cost to operate on Velcro," said Bob, nursing a beer. "The bank froze my account due to an $8,000 charge from West Palm Beach, Florida. It blew through our credit limit. In retrospect, the first unhappy moment was keeping him the extra month down there. The second was the cost overrun." He paused and looked at me. "Actually, the credit card issue was the third unhappy moment. The fact that the horse lived was the second one."

I remained mute.

Meanwhile, Velcro rehabbed in beautiful West Palm for a discounted price of $1,200 per month. After three months, he came home to Ohio sporting a well-healed scar right down the middle of his belly.

Bob looked for levity. "You can hardly see the incision. Those Palm Beach vets probably double as plastic surgeons. Maybe that explains my eight grand."

Within a month of coming home, Jennie rode Velcro. To everybody's glee, nothing fell out of his abdomen. Sarah returned to Ohio and visited. She was no longer interested in riding the horse since he was structurally damaged goods.

Bob and Jennie discovered why colic surgery is a bad idea. If the horse does not die, it lives on as a broken doughnut. Every prospective buyer will balk at buying a horse that has colicked and worse yet, been operated on. Conventional wisdom says that something bad will happen again and nobody will take a chance.

Bob's virtual 40 grand disappeared faster than the West Palm vets. Jennie rode the horse at first level into the summer then was able to sell him to a hunter-jumper girl for $12,000; the same price they paid for him.

Bob raised his eyebrows and offered a sympathetic look. "Jennie was thrilled to get the 12 grand, since to her, it meant we broke even on the horse."

And *that's* Equinomics.

Happy horsin'.

CHAPTER 4

Origins: The Horse Boyfriend

Hello, boys. Today we explore our humble origins. Since one-hundred percent of horse husbands started as boyfriends, logic dictates we ask how we morph from normal boys to submissive men. My friend Louis, a college-age horse boyfriend, tells his story.

***

As a senior in college in 1976, I had rugby buddies at a school in the south. Spring break came and I made the trip from the frozen Midwest to blossoming Dixie in my '66 beetle. The dogwoods were in full bloom, and the campus smelled like perfume. A far cry from the black snow and automobile fumes of Ohio, I knew I had arrived in Eden.

I stayed at the Sig Ep house. One night at a party I spotted Karen, a Tri-Delt. Elegant as a whippet and with the angelic face of Olivia Newton-John, guys worshipped her every move, and I was no exception. Aloof, she expressed disdain for the noisy party, second class furniture, and even the plastic beer cups. I knew my chances with her were non-existent. Hell, I was a scruffy rugby player, adorned with an untrimmed beard, torn rugby trunks, and flip-flops. She was Glinda, the good witch of the south, back-lit by golden rays of sunshine. I could only stare in admiration at the unreachable.

Boys tried to impress her with their rugby stories, drinking skills, and other macho exploits, receiving a roll of the eyes at best, or a wave of the hand, at worst. I listened, an unremarkable salmon in a stream of hopeful spawners.

She turned to her two friends. "Can we get outta here?" The little sycophants nodded in unison. They prepared to leave.

Figuring I had nothing to lose, I raised my eyebrows in mild interest. "So Karen, you don't like any of this. What then, do you like?"

She gave me a who's-the-grub look; a mixture of contempt and overwhelming boredom.

"Well, for your information, dressage." She stretched out the last word like an upper-class southern belle, dres-sahh-ge, with a tiny lilt at the end, adding a soft "ah."

Disheveled and immature, but not dumb, I knew what dressage was. I spotted a big button to push.

"Oh, right, dress-edge. Isn't that the study of proper attire for riding horses? Like, the right way to dress?" I bobbled my head and tacked on a big grin just for fun.

Anger flashed in those gorgeous eyes, the perfect cheeks glowed crimson.

"Asshole." And she stormed out with her little entourage.

"That went well," said a Sig Ep who heard the encounter.

"Indeed, but like politics, bad publicity is better than no publicity. I'm sure she likes me."

"Forget 'er. She's unreachable." I did, returning to my buddies and the beer.

Spring break in South Carolina had been two weeks earlier, so late in March, spring quarter was well underway. In the morning, a Friday, I went for a jog, timing it for a mid-afternoon class change, so I could ogle the girls. As I skimmed along the sidewalk, I spotted the most gorgeous figure in the tightest pair of pants I had ever seen. She walked with knee-high, tight black leather boots aside two other girls, equally attired. I slowed to a strategic pace, keeping a respectful distance, imagining many things. *Oh my. Should I transfer here for my last six weeks?*

A building on the right caught my eye. Horseheads looking at me! The top half of Dutch doors were open, and the critters stared out. Unbeknownst to me, I was looking at the magnificent red-brick and white-columned equestrian facility of the well-endowed school. As I gawked, I missed the fact that the girls had stopped to enter the place. I ran right into the rear end of my dream girl and almost knocked her down.

"Hey!"

I jumped back, embarrassed. "Oh, sorry, I wasn't paying attention."

My perfect girl turned and the fantasy vaporized. Karen glared at me. "You!"

"Oh boy. Yeah me." *But you* do *look good from behind.*

"What do you think you're doing?"

Enjoying the view, thinking things I will never tell you, and oh, I am not sorry. "I was running and got distracted by that building with the horses. What is it anyway? A barn?"

She sighed and offered an exasperated look. "It is our equestrian facility if you must know."

Ah, that made sense. I nodded and raised an eyebrow. "For dressage?" This time I said it right.

Her face relaxed, her eyes softened. "Why, yes." I would later discover this was the first time any boy on campus had ever asked about her passion.

With lovely blue eyes, shoulder-length strawberry blond hair, and a perfect little nose, her prettiness burst forth. My heart flipped. I had to impress her.

With no plan, I forged ahead. "Is your horse stabled here?" This exhausted everything I knew about horses, including blind speculation that she brought a horse to college. A rugby game caused me less trepidation than this conversation.

She raised her perfect eyebrows and tilted her head. I thought I would have a heart attack, such was her beauty. *God, do not let me faint.* "He is. His name is Vader and he's sixteen."

I wondered if the way to a woman's heart was through her horse. That felt pornographic, so I skipped to the next thought. *Be polite*, my limbic system screamed. *Who cares how old he is, and how long do they live anyway?* "Would you be willing to show Vader to me. I would love to see him." Perhaps the biggest lie of my life for the oldest reason in the world.

Still not sold on my interest, she looked skeptical. "Seriously?"

Breathing again, I gave it all I had and made direct eye contact. "Yes. Seriously."

She shrugged and turned, waving me forward. "What's your name, anyway?"

I almost blew it, saying, "Anyway, but you can call me Louis. I'm from Ohio."

She did not react. "Well, I'm Karen."

We entered the gigantic, twenty-four stall barn, built in the shape of an inverted "Y". Three wings consisted of eight stalls each, while the center hub housed an administrative area with separate tack, meeting, and locker rooms, as well as an office. The building, and the forty-acre tract upon which it sat, were donated by a wealthy alumnus family, their picture enshrined in the lobby.

Karen turned to me and smiled. "This way, Louis."

Thump went my heart. Shocked speechless at her gentle demeanor, I stumbled forward, the other two girls giggling at my obvious confusion.

I smelled horse smells, hay, and wood chips, as I walked down the spotless middle aisle, wondering if there was something in the air that changed girls like Karen.

At the end of the aisle were two gigantic doors, open to a lush green pasture with black fencing beyond. As I followed my new true love toward the doors, she stopped at an open area on the left, in which stood the biggest white horse I had ever seen. He had on a headpiece that was clipped to ropes attached to the walls. I learned later he was wearing a halter and was in the cross ties. Grooms working for the barn had prepared him for Karen's arrival.

She planted a big kiss on his nose. "Say hi to Vader."

I thought, unhygienic as it was, I would still kiss her lips, but my passion slipped a notch.

Standing two feet from the big horse, I mumbled a greeting, feeling like a geek.

"Louis, don't be such a chicken, come here and pet him."

Not sure if any girl was worth this, I moved forward and placed a reluctant hand on his neck. "Hi, Vader."

"Louis, come on, you can stand closer."

Oh, the price of love. I crept up to within a couple of inches of his head and patted gently between his eyes. "Hi, Vader."

He brought his head slowly upward, then released the biggest, wettest, nose-rattling snort I had ever heard. The power of his lungs was such that he sprayed my face and glasses with some kind of horse liquid. I jerked back, as the girls melted into hysterics, and Vader nodded his head up and down as if to say, "you deserved it for those naughty thoughts about Karen."

My dignity gone, I croaked. "Men's room?"

Taking a break from the joys of my misfortune, one girl, through tears and wet gulps of laughter, pointed. Slinking away, I removed my glasses, recognizing they had protected my eyes from the noxious goop. I found the john and de-gunked. Less cocky, I returned to Vader and the girls.

Karen met me as I approached the wash stall. Offering a warm smile and extending her hands, she said. "Welcome to horses. How much longer will you be here?"

I discovered that day that I would always be number two, behind a horse, but didn't mind. I also found the most delightful, organized, fussy, and compulsive soulmate. Forty years later and she's made me both happy and a better man. I just needed to learn to speak horse. She also learned a little rugby along the way.

***

So boys, the sooner you accept second chair behind her babies, the easier it will be. Remember, happiness is in the horse of the beholder, and as a horse husband, you will always be the holder.

Happy horsin'.

CHAPTER 5
Injuries: Legends of the Falls

Hello, boys. Today we look at the downside of horses. Injuries. Germane to this discussion is a fundamental rule: when a human is hurt by a horse, the horse is never at fault. If she is tossed from the saddle, kicked, bit, or otherwise traumatized, the horse will be seen to have been reacting to some external force: a windy day, a barking dog, a bug bite, *your* red jacket.

I do not agree with this stance. If they can be taught piaffe and to follow commands with *two* bits in their mouth, they can, by God, be taught to behave. Horse wives reading this recognize why I would not be an effective horse trainer.

Regardless of the reasons for horses to hurt our women, one fact is clear: make sure your wife has health insurance. Sooner or later she will need it. And it does not matter if she is riding; just being around horses is risky. In our horse neighborhood in Aiken, at least five women in five years have sustained major orthopedic or surgical horse-related injuries while not riding. Three were kicked, one got crunched in a stall by a pivoting horse rump, and one lost a thumb to a snap of twisted reins. The number of the infirmed doubles if we add trauma from falls.

Some boast about their injuries. I'm told about one horse wife who came to a Christmas party on crutches. She had surgery after a kick broke her leg. A plastic tube draining the surgical site emerged from the dressing. It was connected to a clear collection bottle that she flashed around like a badge of honor. At least the fluid was red, fitting the decorative motif of the party.

Compared to horses, rugby is safer. I played for nine seasons and only suffered a broken nose, although once I thought I had been gelded. My wife, half my size and twice as tough and a horsewoman for the better part of 30 years, has had more injuries than my entire rugby club, and this includes misbehaving at parties after a game.

There was the broken foot from being stepped on by an eighteen-hundred-pound gelding. We spent that particular Thanksgiving in the emergency room getting x-rayed, splinted, and crutched.

Early on in her riding career, she got tossed a few times. Younger and thus made of rubber, she bounced, but did not break.

"Get back up there! Ya' can't let the lesson end on a fall!" encouraged the asinine trainer. My little wife would scamper back on and finish the lesson. The next day, bruised and stiff, she could not wait to ride again.

Less so now. Trauma necessitates rest and recovery. As we age, our pliable cartilage, tendons, and bones slowly morph into glass; stress them and they break. Had the big horse stepped on her when she was younger, I'm sure her foot would have stretched and not snapped.

My wife's most serious tumble involved being launched off a runaway horse. It left her with a shoulder injury necessitating arthroscopy. Occurring just before a planned trip to Sweden with her sisters, she got her procedure, put the sore arm in a sling, and joined the group. Unfortunately, she could not sleep for the pain and could not remember the trip for the Ambien. After a year of physical therapy, she got back in the saddle ready for more.

In our house, coming off a horse has not been limited to the wife. I am the proud owner of three horse falls. Many years ago, I took reining lessons from my friend, and championship reiner, Ollie. Once, while cantering a twenty-meter circle, I flew off the horse and landed in a heap. Curiously, I was still in the saddle. The cinch had broken.

Ollie could not stop laughing. "By God Stan, that's the first time I ever saw anybody fall off a horse and stay in the saddle!" He never told me to "get back on," not that I could given the state of the equipment.

My second fall resulted from an attempt to ride in an English saddle. These saddles are like miniature wallets laid across the back of the horse. There is not one big enough to accommodate my bulky pelvis and, unlike my western saddle, there is no horn to grab. The spill came during an evening lesson with Ollie.

"Stan, tonight you're gonna find out how strong yer wife's thighs are."

Oh boy, I thought, unsure of where Ollie fit in.

He smiled as he tossed the tiny saddle onto the horse. "Yer gonna learn to post." Up to that point, "post" was a term usually followed by office or cereal, or preceded by fence. I discovered that night it is also a free-standing word for very tired thighs.

I first sat the trot and became very uncomfortable with the relentless gonadal assault from below.

Ollie laughed at my grimaces. "Lift your butt with each stride."

I did, and my center felt much better. However, soon I had a burning sensation in my thighs that overwhelmed my strength. Too tired to continue posting, I dropped back into the saddle. Out of sync with the horse, I lost the rhythm, flew into the air and clunked on the ground.

Ollie roared with laughter. "Ya dropped when ya shoulda lifted and he popped you right out. Never seen it so smooth."

Unhurt, I stood, dusted off and suggested a beer. Once Ollie dried his eyes, he agreed. Further rides were limited to western saddles, where there is more padding in the seat and the trot is not so rough. I also "posted" new respect for my wife's thighs.

My third fall occurred in Florida. Vigert (vee-gurt), an eighteen-hand teddy bear, would wait next to the fence for me to give him a treat. My wife rode the gentle giant, and he always behaved under saddle. He seemed easy-going and nice, but I realized later that my relationship with him was driven by food. I misinterpreted his kind demeanor for friendship.

On the fatal day, he stood next to a four-rail fence in a paddock that was nothing but sand. I looked up at him. "Dude, I'll bet I can climb this fence, slip on to your back, and walk you around."

He continued to stand, which I interpreted as consent.

Using the fence as a ladder, I reached the top and threw my left leg over his back. Since he had neither bit nor halter, I grabbed some mane for leverage. He continued to stand. Once I had my balance, I left the safety of the fence and rode bareback from what seemed like six floors above the ground.

The ride lasted two strides. Once he had my full weight, he bolted to canter and on the third step dropped his head and bucked. Launched from a catapult, I landed ass-over-teakettle in the sand. After he off-loaded me, he turned, stood, and stared.

My wife caught the commotion and rushed around the corner to check on the fuss. She made it just in time to see the stupendous buck and my impromptu aerial.

"What the *hell* are you doing?"

I recall she did not ask after my health.

I stood and brushed sand off my butt. "Just thought I'd take a short ride."

"Without tack? No helmet? And are you wearing flip-flops?"

I looked down. "Well, I figured with no stirrups, I wouldn't need shoes."

"God! Have you lost your mind? Are you okay?"

Finally. "I'm fine."

She shook her head, entered the paddock and walked toward the horse. "You probably scared him half to death." *But what about me?* I whined inside, learning yet again about horses, husbands, and priorities.

Even as I write this, I have no idea what possessed me to do such a crazy thing. I did learn that a quiet horse getting a treat at the fence does not translate into a docile bareback ride. I have also taken "riding bareback" off my bucket list.

Injuries are not limited to humans doing stupid things. Some horses fit the category. Rugger, our very first baby and the product of a cross between a good stallion and a cranky mare, was obnoxious and smart. Doing things no normal horse would do got him into trouble on a regular basis.

One spring day in Ohio, I walked toward his paddock where he met me at the fence, signifying a good mood. On this occasion, he poked his nose toward me looking for a treat. I caught a hideous, fecal odor.

My wife joined me and I turned to her. "Have you noticed how bad that horse stinks?"

She leaned toward him and took a sniff. "Oh, yuck. What did he get into?"

"If he was a dog, I'd say a dead fish or cat poop, but he's supposed to eat grass."

I entered the paddock, haltered him and held his head. I grabbed and raised his floppy upper lip. The stink was his breath. The front tooth dangled, loosely imbedded in mushy red gums that were swollen and weeping.

My wife stared, shocked. "Oh my God, what happened?"

"Looks like he tore out a tooth and infected his gums." Suppressing a gag, I pulled away.

We called the vet. He wired the tooth back into place and gave antibiotics. The stink cleared, but three days later the wire was hanging out his mouth and the tooth was missing, replaced by a huge gaping hole between his front teeth. He looked like a hillbilly.

The vet offered a theory. "He probably was chewing a nail on a fence post. The nail head may have gotten caught behind the tooth, startling him and making him jerk his head. The nail stayed in the post and the tooth ripped out. Then the whole mess got infected."

The horse recovered and remained obnoxious for the next 18 years.

So, in the equestrian world, both people and horses can get hurt. For your wife, most injuries are driven by her unrelenting passion for the critters. For husbands, most accidents result from random events or generalized stupidity. The latter tracks to my Vigert adventure. Thinking about it, my flip-flops proved prophetic, Vigert flipped, I flopped.

Happy horsin'.

CHAPTER 6

Of Manure & Metamucil

Hello, boys. Let's talk manure.

First, horse husbands perceive manure differently than horse wives: we do not think it smells good, and it suggests waste, not the affirmation of what is now a happier horse. On the other hand, we will concede that stooling is way better than colicking (a term found on the internet, but not in my dog-eared 1974 dictionary).

Any discussion of manure has to start with anatomy, and there is a lot of it. According to Wikipedia, the intestinal tract of a one thousand pound horse is one hundred feet long and may store up to fifty gallons of what I consider to be distasteful liquid. One gallon of water weighs about 8.3 pounds, so we are talking about *four hundred* pounds of potential poop. If you have ever mucked a stall, this number will not surprise you. But the amazing thing about all horses, and their ever-efficient bowels, is that they can turn light, fluffy, one hundred dollar bills, into heavy wet manure. How does *that* work? It feels like quantum mechanics (see Chapter 3, Equinomics).

When you think about it, it's a minor miracle that owners of several horses do not always have some horse colicking. If each horse has one hundred feet of bowel, it only takes three animals to have a football field's worth of "colic-able" gut. I don't understand how they *cannot* colic.

Perhaps it is because horse wives in the know (like mine) give their horses Metamucil every month. My apologies in advance, for if your horse wife is not giving the herd monthly Metamucil, and she reads this article, she will soon start. This means that when shopping at Costco, you will buy Metamucil by the fifty-five-gallon drum and the check out girl will think you own a nursing home. And do not bother telling her it's for horses, she will be skeptical—as as if you told her you look at *Playboy* for the articles. On the upside, our horses like Metamucil. It gives them orange lips and fresh fruity breath. I guess it is good for them. My wife says it is, so it is.

There is another basic rule about colic—it will never happen if your wife is home, but the likelihood skyrockets if she goes out of town. The odds reach near certainty if she has left the feeding chores to you. Here is why I know this. In spring 1997, we moved to our first horse farm in Ohio. That decision, by the way, eliminated all vacations as a couple, and she would not leave the farm for another 30 months. Alas, however, she did eventually sally forth. She visited her twin in Albuquerque over Super Bowl weekend. I thought, no problem. I had been well-schooled in my expected duties, we had a day girl who handled the chores, and my wife would only be gone Friday through Monday. What could possibly go wrong?

I was on call that weekend but expected things to cool by Sunday night and the six P.M. kick-off of the football game. January in central Ohio is cold, and always dark by four in the afternoon. Rolling home around five, a tiny feeling of trepidation clawed in my chest. Why are the lights on in the barn? Drawing closer, I saw a vet's truck parked at the open end of the barn and all stall lights glimmering in the clear, fifteen-degree evening. A feeling of deep dread overwhelmed me. I grew concerned for the fate of my marriage. Unlike the latter, the horse could be replaced.

I parked and entered the barn where I discovered a horrifying scene: a guy was standing on a step ladder and pouring clear, steaming liquid from a one-gallon jug down a monster tube protruding from a horse's nose. My barn girl gripped a lead line to the halter, while the vet's assistant held a huge blue funnel at the mouth of the tube. The wide eyes of the mare suggested unhappiness to me, but mild sedation kept her docile. They were just finishing this grisly task when I came in.

Our barn girl turned to me. "When I was cleanin' stalls she grunted a bunch and pawed the ground. It looked like colic so I called the vet."

The vet looked at me with a practiced eye. "Yep, coulda' been colic. We sedated, intubated, then gave a gallon of warm mineral oil. That oughtta' do it. Just walk 'er till she stools. Amanda, go ahead and pull the tube."

Amanda pulled out the big rubber snake, gathered all remaining equipment, and followed the vet to the truck. He slammed closed the back as she jumped into the front seat.

"I'll send a bill. Good luck." And he was gone. I found out later that he and Amanda (his wife) had a Super Bowl party to attend.

When I turned around, I watched our barn girl pull away

in her car. Waving, she called. "I'll be back in the morning, I'm goin' to a Super Bowl party." It seemed everyone got an invitation but me.

In five short minutes, I was deep in the woods, alone with the clogged horse we were boarding as a favor, freezing my ass off, and most unhappy about the vaporization of my unremarkable Super Bowl plans.

However, being both a guy and a resilient horse husband, I quickly identified some options. I first called Tim, the now-a-schmuck owner. I was told he was at a Super Bowl party. Right. All I knew was that he was not at my Super Bowl party.

The vigil began. At periodic intervals, I walked the horse around the twelve by twelve stall. The animal, by the way, seemed fine. Between walks I sat in my golf cart in the unheated barn just outside the stall, wrapped in musty horse blankets as a defense against the now eight-degree night, and watched the Super Bowl on a tiny black and white television. Like a car on a precipice, it was balanced on the dash of the cart. For fear of toppling the TV, I was a church mouse and tippy-toed every time I got on or off the cart's bench. I most certainly did not belch or fart.

Midway through the third quarter, I heard the reassuring plop of success, followed by a visual and pungent confirmation. Good horsey!

I gathered my stuff faster than the vet and prepared to head up to the house. At that moment, Tim arrived. Somebody had paged him about his horse. He took over the now unnecessary vigil.

Having dodged the proverbial colic bullet, as well as a

future divorce attorney, I hustled back to the warmth of the house, thawed out, and enjoyed the last two minutes of the game. My wife returned the next day from a wonderful trip to New Mexico. I went back to work thinking that horses were not a good idea. The mare, by the way, had no further problems, although she probably had no love lost for the guy who tubed her and dumped in a gallon of mineral oil.

At the other end of the colic spectrum, is no colic and the steady production of manure. This leads to a new decision: what do you do with all that poop? First, you muck stalls, and before you even think about starting, you will not do it right. You will miss at least one turd, and you will throw away too many wood chips with each fork full, thus wasting bedding. You will also not remove all urine-soaked chips, rendering the floor of the stall unhygienic. This is similar to trying to sterilize an outhouse. Completing your task, you will find the pull cord for dragging the damn manure bucket draped inside and buried in a yucky mix. You will not discover this fact until the bucket is full and you are thinking "that was not so bad." I will not explain how to extract the cord from the gamish (Yiddish for mixture or mishmash. Perfect term)—suffice to say this is why your gloves are now wet on the inside and stink.

Once manure is out of the stall, it either goes into a pile somewhere or into a spreader. We spread. By the way, be careful with manure buckets, they are tapered at the bottom, are always overfilled by helpful horse husbands, and invariably fall over as you drag them to the spreader. The only thing worse than shoveling manure once is shoveling it twice.

Actually, there is something worse than shoveling it

twice—chopping it, and then shoveling it twice. Our first winter at the Ohio farm, and when we were low on the learning curve, I dumped wet manure into a spreader where it froze into granite. I ran the spreader and snapped the chain that propelled stuff backward. Well done. I stared at a very big spreader with a huge load of frozen manure. Determined not to wait three months for the stuff to thaw, I got the ax and *chopped* manure, depositing the product of my efforts into manure buckets to be dragged away. No matter how you twist it, chopping manure will always be a horse husband's job, so rather than debate it, avoid it.

So that's poop in a nutshell. Remember, manure happens, and it is serious business:

Don't frolic if there's colic,
Don't skip a dirty stall.
Don't argue over money,
Don't even joke at all.
Happy bowel makes happy horse,
And leads to happy wife, of course.

Happy horsin'.

CHAPTER 7

Hay Ho, Nobody Home

Hello, boys. No, the title of this essay does not contain a typographic error, hay is the topic. Remember when you thought hay was dry grass clippings or the same as straw? Early on, we all thought that way, but not now.

When it comes to hay, a non-horse husband or boyfriend will say and do things that miss the mark. For example, we were in a tack store in Aiken and my wife was looking at stirrup leathers and a girth pad. I was hanging around waiting since there is nothing in a tack store that interests me. Sort of like fabric stores or the Yankee Candle Company, nothing resonates.

Twenty minutes into my wait, a guy burst into the store and yelped at the clerk. "How much for a bale of hay?"

She looked at him. "Ten dollars for orchard."

"Thanks." He scurried out.

It was obvious he was no horse husband, nor horse anything. His question was like going into a women's shoe store and asking, "How much for a pair of shoes?" Perhaps he was a guy trying to impress a horse girl with his vast knowledge of the economics of hay. If he gets anywhere with her, it won't be because of hay.

Through osmosis, I have learned about hay. First, hay is not straw. Straw is used for bedding when waiting for your mare to foal. It's also the same stuff the electric company puts down to prevent erosion after stripping a forest for a new power line. Second, hay is grass and according to the internet, there are about twelve-thousand grass species, including grassland grasses, and curiously, bamboo. We do not feed our horses bamboo.

A few types of common horse hays include orchard, coastal, and timothy. We (my wife) like timothy or timothy mixes. Horse wives know the nutritional value, estimated caloric output, fiber per pound, and approximate post-digestive methane content of every bite. I do not, but respect the depth of such knowledge. I have learned that fescue causes abortions in pregnant mares and that too much alfalfa makes horse ankles "stock up", a vague veterinary term for swelling.

Our hay comes in square bales. The older you are, the heavier the bale. When we lived in Ohio, we baled our own hay. We had a hay farmer, Dan, who did the cutting and the baling. He did it for "free" since we gifted him the 1,200 extra bales. We had 14 acres and got a lot of hay. I am pretty sure it was timothy with a smattering of alfalfa. I could ask my wife, but the question might annoy her since I should know the answer.

Hay farmers in Ohio have it tough. Since Dan could only cut hay between May and September, he either worked frenetically when there was good weather or sat around waiting for good weather. We were dependent on Dan to cut the hay for our horses so his delays became our delays. In March, hearty new growth would pop up despite the snow, and by late spring, the first cutting was ready. Unfortunately for us, he'd start with his big-money customers, 100 acres or more, waiting on our pipsqueak farm until the end. By the time he got to us, it usually rained, so we would have to wait.

When the time came, our fields would get mowed, the fodder laid down in neat rows across the green pastures to dry before baling. Then it would rain, ruining the crop and we would have to wait several weeks for the next cutting. Other years it never rained, and we baled brittle stalks. Regardless of the quality of the hay, we were last on the list. Dan's baler usually had plenty of miles on it by the time he got to us, and nine times out of ten, the machine would break, giving another delay, and more hay-angst.

After seven years, we left Ohio and the hay hassles behind. Unfortunately, we traded Ohio for northern Florida, where there is only sand, sand colic, and no decent hay. We had to buy our hay in Ocala, two hours away. Costing 50 bucks a bale and each weighing 120 pounds, the bales came six to a pallet. The weight of each bale seemed to increase as I grunted and groaned with unloading. The hay guys in Ocala used a forklift to load a pallet into our horse trailer. I did not have a forklift. You get the picture.

Ohio has winter, which means all organisms living outside have to die, hibernate, or fly south. Florida does not have winter. Florida cools a little between October and March but is otherwise a gigantic warm incubator, allowing mind-boggling numbers of bacteria, fungi, and insects to proliferate. From April onward, these pests emerge, invading everything. You could not only smell the fungus, you could hear it growing. The hot muggy summers turned the air into a sticky sauna, and like an under chlorinated, too-warm swimming pool, we spawned colonies of algae, but this time on our million-dollar hay bales.

My wife caught it first. "Do the bales look blue to you?" I had never thought about the color of a bale, only their weight—heavy.

"Ah, I guess." Then I looked. She was right, there was a blue film on the surface of each bale.

She pointed and wrinkled her nose. "I think we have algae on our hay."

"We just bought it. It wasn't blue then."

"It's blue now. We have algae. They can't eat this."

Even *I* thought our horses shouldn't eat algae. This meant "fresh bales" and more frequent trips to Ocala for smaller loads, so our babies could eat the hay before the algae did. For the first time, I appreciated Ohio winters. This also provides more reasons why we love Aiken; enough winter to kill the algae, lighter bales, and of critical importance, the hay place delivers.

Another general comment on hay. No matter where you live, if you get within ten feet of a bale, you will get little bits of the stuff under your shirt or in your socks. I don't know how this happens without direct contact, but it does. This leads me to a broader theme; never wear anything but barn clothes to the barn. Never (see Chapter 2).

Your barn clothes can be fancy or simple, but they should only be worn in the barn and *not* in the house. I can ramble on about horse stink, wood chips, manure, and other unwanted materials, but will not. Suffice to say, identify barn clothes, keep them in an airlock or your garage, and use them. Despite what your wife says, you are in fact, cleaner than a horse. Like Custer, this is your last stand. If you lose, get a divorce.

But, back to the hay. Despite its great smell and the love the horses have for it, hay is messy. Once you cut the twine that holds the bale together, it may explode. If not, then the flakes that constitute the bale will come out thick, thin, compressed or loose, but never perfect. "Giving a flake" translates to a little or a lot of hay.

A more abstract concept is the half-a-flake. This is less precise than the women's shoe question. Ever try to tear one? They do not tear. If you are lucky, it may come apart without degenerating into a bunch of loose hay, but in general, flakes do not de-flake gracefully. When the tear leaves a loose mess, scoop up what you can, toss it over the fence and call it a half. Don't worry about it. If it's cold, she will feel sorry for them anyway and give them another flake in an hour or two. You will still get credit for the feeding.

Flakes also do not transport well. Every guy has tried to move a flake from the bale to a stall by carrying it and invariably trails a stream of loose strands across the floor of the barn. You leave it; it's not *that* much.

But she's watching. "You are wasting hay. You need to rake it up and give the rest of it to Wally."

Do not argue. Rake up the micro-handful of hay and give it to Wally. Next time, distribute hay using the cart with the wheels. You probably already know this. And, if you carried, you'll want to finish raking in a hurry so you can get out of the damn itchy tee shirt.

Some people like to save money by buying a semi-truck-load of hay and then selling it or splitting it between several farms. If you are not the semi buyer, you have to go to the girl's farm and unload your hay into your truck, take it home, and unload it into your barn. This saves money and alleviates the need to work with a tack store that delivers. Since your time is free, your wife is happy about all the money she saved. She is the only happy party. Spend the money, avoid the unloading, and stick with the tack store.

On the other hand, if *you* ordered the semi, there can be issues. First, you do not know what you have until you get it. Moldy? Stemmy? Sorry, you are stuck with all 700 bales. And second, if you park the trailer at your place, you become a landlord for hay, with tenants showing up at all hours to claim their cut. As close as you are to your friends, you have to be there to count bales. You never know, unlike your wife, not all horsewomen are honest.

So, flakey or not, that is a horse husband guide to hay. Of note, the title of this essay comes from a song that includes "hey ho, nobody home, meat, nor drink, nor money have I none." The last point is key. You will both agree that you have no resources, but she will argue that it has nothing to do with horses or fancy hay. It is the result of money squandered on your widescreen TV. Pointing out that she also watches it will not help. A Zen master might say, "You, Grasshopper, are but a flake in a bale, constrained by metaphorical twine, that when cut, allows for short bursts of freedom, only later to be consumed, and converted to manure."

Happy horsin'.

CHAPTER 8

From Teeth to Sheath: Horsey Health Care

Hello, boys. How's your health care? I hope none is needed, but if it is, I hope it is first class. Regardless of *your* status, your wife's horses receive superior health care, including everything from a dentist who makes house calls to the unexplained horse wife obsession with cleaning "the sheath." Not only is it disgusting, it's unfair. When was the last time anybody offered to clean your sheath?

Of course, we are referring to what is the horsey foreskin. Considering the size of a horse, it should be called twelveskin. I am not interested in a deep dive into the equine urinary tract, so will suffice to point out that horsewomen worry about stuff accumulating down there, and (far too) often feel that interventional hygiene is necessary. They perform some unmentionable task, then report to their husbands with the glowing pride of accomplishment, "I cleaned Wally's sheath today, boy, was it dirty."

Sheaths aside, there's a lot of other stuff that can go wrong. In another essay, we explored all 100 feet of bowel and its associated pathology. But what of other organs? How about the heart? Horse hearts can be wife-rated: "Wally is such a good boy, he has such a big heart," or horse husband-rated: "It pumps blood." Let's discuss the latter.

Just how big is a horse heart? It weighs about eight pounds and, depending on how fast it pumps, can move six to 70 gallons of blood per minute (your heart is about ten ounces and pumps one to two gallons per minute, the latter when you are maximally excited with activities perhaps associated with your sheath). The heart of a horse also pumps anywhere from 20 to 220 times per minute. There are valves between the four chambers of a horse heart, and if one valve does not close completely, a murmur (a soft "shush") is heard with each beat. Murmurs, if severe, are easily heard; if mild, they may be subtle and their presence open to interpretation. This is the gap needed by veterinarians to do a little financial pumping of their own.

Vigert was a gigantic (18 hands but looked like 24) warm-blood with the demeanor of a teddy bear (introduced in Chapter 5). For reasons I cannot recall, he was seen by a vet who heard a murmur on examination. My wife and I are both doctors, and we never did hear said murmur. Nevertheless, tests were needed. A leaky heart valve can lead to heart failure. Heart failure is bad in people, unthinkable in horses.

Human heart tests mean a trip to the hospital. Unless you are starring on "My 600 Pound Life," it is likely you would ride in the car and travel a short distance. Unlike you, our horse had to be loaded into the trailer and hauled two hours south to Ocala, and the equine cardiovascular center. This is like the Mayo Clinic for horse hearts.

This place is not just for lethargic Vigerts but also for race-horses, jumpers, eventers, and, like Vigert, pets. Like all large animal care centers, it was a cross between a M.A.S.H. unit and a construction site. There were medical machines and dressing carts scattered between hydraulic lifts, overhead pulleys on rails, and people driving Bearcats with scoops full of poop. In this setting, the loud murmur of activity was unmistakable.

Vigert's room was the size of six stalls. For the racehorses, there was a horse treadmill in one corner. This is not the little human thing you find at your health club, no, this was two horses long, three feet wide, and with heavy metal pipe rails to keep the critter contained on the device. I never saw a horse on the treadmill, but can you imagine its confusion? For the first time, he feels the ground moving beneath, and as the mat speeds up, there is no choice but to walk, trot, or canter. Terrible. Whatever the damn horse has, it does not justify this abuse. But I digress. We were not there for the treadmill.

Vigert's theoretic murmur required a very real echocardiogram which helps determine the severity of leaky valves. I held a docile Vigert with a lead line hooked to his halter. No sedation needed for Vigert, he was born sedated. The test began as the vet moved the acoustic probe around the horse's chest. Once located, we saw the image of his heart (the size of a football) on the screen, pumping at a leisurely 33 beats each minute. The vet and my wife stared at the rhythmic gray shadowing for a minute or two, making murmurs of their own as they scrutinized the fuzzy images. I waited and thought about lunch, which, by the way, was a non-starter. Have you ever tried the Wendy's drive-through while pulling a gooseneck?

After the test ended, Vigert's valves were declared "non-leaky," and unlike the first vet, "highly competent." The echo-cardiographer could not hear the theoretical murmur, but lack of murmur does not mean a free echo, so we forked over the 300 bucks, and left happy in the knowledge that Vigert's valves were fine and his pump would continue to pump.

So, for the cost of the echo, and 60 bucks worth of gas, we learned that at least one of our four horse hearts were fine, that our local vet was a zero, and that horse husbands do not need lunch since they can eat the rest of those baby carrots and almonds that were leftover from the inbound trip.

Horsey health care: good for the horse, bad for the bank, hard on a hungry husband.

Happy horsin'.

CHAPTER 9

Let's Breed

Hello, boys. When my wife and I were younger, we enjoyed breeding. It may be the same with you and your wife, but in this case, I'm referring to horse-breeding. For several years we had a broodmare and enjoyed the trials and tribulations of growing and raising baby horses.

Vanity, a German Hanoverian mare, came to us through a divorce settlement from a girl in Pennsylvania. I don't know what he got, but she got Vanity. Unfortunately, with him went the revenue stream to support the horse and Vanity had to go. My wife jumped in to save the day, buying the horse for a song.

A great mover, Vanity had suffered childhood trauma to a foot, leaving her ambulatory but not competitive. Offering a stellar bloodline, she became a broodmare, similar to poor Queen Victoria, who, despite being one of the greatest monarchs of all time, had nine children. Vanity came close with seven.

With a dream to breed great dressage horses, we envisioned Vanity as the index mother of a future string of stars. To get there, my wife studied horse breeding. She then enrolled in an equine obstetrics course at the Ohio State vet school. Attending every lecture and taking voracious notes, her breadth of knowledge soon eclipsed the instructor. At the time, she was a practicing radiologist and her work included reading ultrasounds.

One day the unsuspecting teacher tackled ultrasonography and its use in equine obstetrics. The students stood in a group surrounding a device about the size of a microwave oven.

The instructor pointed. "This is an ultrasound machine."

My wife noted it was not a very good one, but kept this to herself.

"People radiologists," the instructor continued, "use these to diagnose things like kidney stones or how many eggs a woman may have for ovulation. The ultrasound image is easy to read. A good people radiologist can make a diagnosis in five seconds, then charge a fortune for the interpretation. It's very easy money for them."

My demure wife, standing two rows back, raised her hand and smiled. "Hi. You should know I am one of those 'good people radiologists'."

This shut down the radiology-shaming and forced the red-faced instructor to complete the presentation in record time.

My wife gave a laconic summary. "Her voice was a little shaky, but she had it coming."

Snarky instructors aside, the course proved invaluable and provided needed confidence in taking the breeding mission forward.

The rare husband who reads this is thinking, let's hear about the breeding. Visions of exaggerated masculinity, physical dominance, snorting, etc., flash through his mind. What he is excited about is called "live cover." For his benefit, I will add one colorful but depressing note.

In live cover, a mare, known to be in heat, is at one end of an arena, haltered and held in place by a nervous groom. She (the mare) is wearing a saddle-like cover as protection from aggressive stallion hooves. At this juncture, the mare is biologically ready to go but emotionally could use a little romantic chemistry. Enter the horse with the worst job in the entire animal kingdom, the "teasing stallion." This poor guy's single job is to be led over to a mare preparing to be bred, and turn up the heat. Taking a sniff, he gets the message and rises to the occasion. Their mutual interest generates just the right chemistry, but before actual combustion, the poor son of a bitch is led (dragged?) back to his stall, allowing the actual stallion to come over and combust. Meanwhile, the shunned warm-up guy is left to stand in his stall alone, wondering how it all went wrong. I would speculate that that cranky retired teasing stallions do not make good show horses.

Live coverage, colorful and kinetic as it is, is generally restricted to thoroughbred horse racing and is not the only way to get a baby. You can also "ship." We shipped. I refer to semen shipped frozen from a target stallion's breeding farm. By the way, the life of a stud horse is pretty good; he gets to do live cover, and, to supplement his activities, as well as the breeder's income, he may have his semen collected. Back in 1989, we paid around $200 for a stud fee. The colts who win the Kentucky Derby command a thousand times that.

But, you ask, how does one collect semen from a horse?

A stallion can be taught to mount a "breeding phantom"

with an artificial cavity. Once mounted, he releases and the goods are collected. Small portions are snap-frozen in liquid nitrogen, stored, and shipped to customers when needed.

Frozen semen is sent overnight by Fed Ex in a cleverly termed "equitainer," an insulated blue plastic box. Unlike my wife, who worked at several hospitals, my job was based in a single office, so the samples always came to me.

I would get a page once it arrived. "Dr. Nahman, a big blue box just came for you."

"Thanks, Mary. It's frozen horse semen. Can you put it on my desk?"

There's a long pause. "Ah, should I wear gloves?"

Tired of nervous secretaries, I wanted to say, "No, but whatever you do, do not let it brush against your stomach. Horse sperm are very strong and can travel a long way."

Instead, I opted for civility. "No, Mary, it's just a fancy Fed Ex box. There is no danger."

Before going too far, we need to explore the sources of horse semen. As a radiologist and horse enthusiast, my wife has a great eye for anatomy and how it correlates with horse gaits. In our breeding days, she and her girlfriends would shop for the perfect stallion by getting together to watch "stud films" on videotapes sent from stud owners. I remind the younger readers that *stud film* used to be slang for pornography.

The girls would gather in our basement and watch the videos, assessing each potential sperm donor. One time, I came home from work and called to the basement. "Hey, what are you guys doing down there?"

My wife answered. "We're watching stud films."

She never found the humor in this response, but I did. The hilarity continued once the video rolled and the comments drifted upstairs.

"Oh my, that's a big one."

"Nice back end."

"With his head down, he really pushes from behind."

And my personal favorite. "Look at this view, with the bit in his mouth, he seems to smile when he comes."

Following what was *not* a pornographic session, the girls gave their opinions and my wife made her decision about the future father of our next baby horse.

Studs can make semen daily. Mares ovulate about every three weeks, giving a one- or two-day window for fertilization. You can't just use a calendar, you need a vet to tell you when an egg is ready to pop.

We had a wonderful old-school guy who did all of our inseminating. With Vanity in the cross ties waiting, he would don a rubber glove that went to his shoulder, then slide his hand into her rectum climbing ever forward until he could feel the ovaries through the thin wall of the bowel. Groping around and finding an enlarged egg, he could then give us a window.

"It's Monday, you need the semen tomorrow or no later than Wednesday."

We'd call the breeder, and he would ship a frozen sample. I remember one particular insemination. My wife was working so I met the vet with my big blue box. I already had Vanity in the cross ties when he arrived. He pulled on the glove, this time a sterile one since he was going into her reproductive tract. To inseminate, he would insert the tip of a long, sterile glass pipette into the mare's cervix and using a red rubber bulb on the end, squirt the semen into the uterus.

Easy, right? Here's how it went.

With his left hand clutching the pipette by the red suction bulb, he turned to me.

"Okay, now hand me the bag of semen." He reached with his right hand.

As he did so, we both saw he had an immediate problem. He needed another hand to open the tightly sealed, small baggie with the semen.

"Need help?" I asked, hoping he would say no, but having no other option.

"Nope," and he raised the bag to his mouth and, using his teeth, tore it open. Deftly dipping the pipette into the liquid, he used the red bulb to aspirate the needed volume. After handing the bag back to me, he turned, put his right hand into the mare, inserted the pipette and completed the insemination with a squeeze of the bulb. With that, we were done. I can tell you *I* was done.

I was not sure if I admired his dedication or thought he was crazy. The one thing I was sure was that craved Listerine, and right now.

He called that night. "Bev, don't hold yer breath. I checked the sample and there wasn't a living sperm anywhere. It looked like a bomb went off. You'll need to call the breeder and arrange for another sample in three weeks so we can try again."

A developing horse fetus can be detected about two weeks after the insemination, so just to be sure, he visited again to feel the uterus. Depressed, we stood awaiting the grim verdict.

With his hand in Vanity's rectum, he felt around, his face contorted with concentration. Then out came the arm, and he turned to us. "Well Bev, I believe the Pope is Chinese. Don't know how it happened, but she's pregnant."

Eleven months later, Vanity delivered. That adventure is detailed in the next chapter, so don't go away.

Happy horsin', rubber bulb and all.

CHAPTER 10

Deliverance

Hello, boys. In a previous chapter, we went through the grisly business of getting our horse, Vanity, pregnant. Things now escalate as we deliver the product of that success, a 110 pound bundle of joy.

You shrug your shoulders and say to me, but never to your wife, "What's the big deal? Horses have been having babies without our help for eons." True, but since we don't have statistics on horse infant mortality in the wild, maybe they *do* need us. Also, with today's selective breeding, some babies may be bigger than nature intended, necessitating a "little" help with the delivery. But, your concern about the term little is otherwise valid. Nothing about horses is little, except maybe attention spans and horse treats.

We wonder if all our coddling, supplements, and scripted diets have made a difference in horse life spans. The answer is on Cumberland Island, where the wild horses roam free. Average lifespan, about ten years. Ours stick around for 20 or 30.

The Cumberland horses are small and scruffy, with untrimmed hooves that curl at the toes. I am certain they also harbor intestinal worms competing for ingested calories. You may know people like this, complete with worms, and they don't last long either. Good food, hygiene, and medicine help both horses and humans. To this list, I will add help with delivering babies.

My friend Bob, from the Equinomics chapter, and I were discussing horses over a beer at his golf club. With a shake of his head, he reached for some popcorn. "Jennie wants to breed her mare. How long does it take?"

He meant the gestational period. "Three hundred and forty days, or about 11 months."

"God, that's worse than people. Is the horse pissy the whole time?"

"Depends on the mare, but they do gain weight."

"Well, at least I know what to expect. What happens at delivery?"

"The water breaks and it's like Hoover Dam letting go; I always wear knee-high rubber boots."

Bob turned green and pushed his beer away. "I think I've had enough."

Feeling snarky, I continued. "But dude, you oughta see the placenta. This thing is…" His eyes bugged out, and with a chop of his hand, he cut me off and left the table.

Well, he asked.

Insemination strategies are unusual in people but are vital with regard to horses. For us, inseminating the mare in late April was smart. The foal was on the ground eleven months later in March, just as spring is warming. Likewise, fertilizing the mare anytime in February made no sense; who needs a shivering foal in the dead of winter?

The eleven-month gestational period offers time for preparation. For horse wives, this begins the day the pregnancy is confirmed by the vet. As soon as we found out, she started working on her delivery list. Sitting in the tack room with pen in hand, the former radiologist drilled me with her eyes. This must have been how a chest x-ray felt when she was reading films.

She ticked off items with her fingers. "We need to up Vanity's hay and grain, get straw for the foaling stall, and arrange to sleep in the barn at least three weeks before delivery."

Not seized with the same compulsion, I just looked at her. "We have 326 days to go." She waved me off, returning to her list.

By day 300, even I could tell Vanity was pregnant. Much bigger and with veins coursing her belly, she was a monster of a horse as she lumbered around the frozen paddock. Two weeks later, barn nights for my wife began. She catnapped in a room adjacent to the foaling stall while Vanity munched hay.

Despite sleep deprivation, my wife remained intense. "Every time Vanity snorted, I got up and checked. I thought her water had broken or she had laid down to start pushing."

"Can I help?"

Her withering look gave the answer, so I stayed in the house, close to the phone.

Around 1 A.M. on day 341, the phone rang, rousing me from a deep sleep.

"Ah, yeah, hullo?"

"Get out here. Her water just broke."

"Who's this?" But she had hung up.

Realizing my marriage was teetering on termination, I jumped out of bed, dressed, and hustled to the barn. Clad in a coat over a tee shirt tucked into long pants and knee-high rubber boots, I arrived less to fanfare than irritation.

"Where have you been?" I had been awake for three minutes.

Clad in similar garb, my wife led me into the stall. Vanity stopped pacing and stood. We sloshed across the wet straw of the twelve by eighteen foot enclosure.

She lifted the mare's tail for a peek. "Look, a hoof." Now *that* was weird. Wrong structure, wrong place. *Oh, Bob, you'd love this.*

Vanity seemed comfortable just standing. Then she made a slow but definitive move toward laying down. Carrying an extra 300 pounds made her wobble as she clunked to the floor. Within a few minutes, she laid on her side and made small grunting noises.

Our hoof made progress and by one-thirty, another appeared, the top one longer than the new one. After 15 more minutes, not too much had happened.

My boss pointed at protruding hooves. "It's too slow, and Vanity is getting tired. Grab them, and start pulling."

Now fully awake, I squatted, grabbed one hoof with each hand and gave a tug. Nothing.

"Wait for a contraction."

The mare pushed, I pulled. After a couple of push-pull cycles, I heated up and took off my barn coat. The protruding hooves were slippery with some unthinkable substance; already my gloves were soaked and destined for the garbage.

My wife leaned in. "It's coming, keep pulling."

Babies come out in this order: hoof, hoof, head, shoulder, horse.

After five minutes of pulling, the head and shoulder cleared, and zot! a brown bundle squirted out and laid motionless on the straw. Then, the head bobbed as the front legs flailed and the baby freed itself from the amniotic sac. The back legs flexed and before us was a little horse laying in the straw. At the same time, Vanity sat up and craned her head back, nickering nose-to-nose with the foal.

"Whew." My exhausted wife looked worse than Vanity. But business remained. She took inventory. "Four legs, two ears, two eyes. Oh, look at the little white star between its eyes. Isn't it cute?"

Maybe it was, but my favorite tee shirt from Carmel had been slimed. It would follow the gloves to the garbage after fifty failed attempts to wash out the off-white dingy stain.

"Let her nuzzle and bond with the baby."

As if I had plans to do anything but change my shirt.

My wife turned to leave the stall. "I'll get the antiseptic for the umbilical stump."

As expected, the cord separated when the baby came out, the vessels retracting into the baby and leaving a short remnant dangling from his belly. Returning with supplies, she completed cleaning the nubbin of tissue and ushered me out the door.

"Let's give them some quiet time. Then you can help the baby stand and nurse."

I got the first part about standing but was less sure about my role with the second.

After an hour, Vanity wobbled up and stood, then gave a

good shake. I helped the rickety baby colt stand, finishing off my tee shirt. The little guy, slippery but cooperative, stumbled around semi-drunk. I hunched behind as the spotter, offering support or corrections in balance as needed. We estimated him at 110 pounds, 80 of which were legs. The back legs in particular, were thick and looked strong. I prayed he did not kick and make me a gelding.

As the baby and I found our way around the stall, his balance improved. Vanity waited for him to find the Promised Land and start nursing. I moved it along, guiding his head to a waiting nipple. His mouth already smacking on auto-suck, he stood on his own and nursed.

Throughout, the mare seemed fine, except for the pink-white cord hanging out her rear and dragging in the straw. That cable-like bundle of vessels, the diameter of my wrist, led up to the placenta or afterbirth, which she passed an hour later. I collected the product so my wife could inspect it.

Irregularities or missing pieces necessitated an immediate call to the vet.

Crouching, my wife gave the 20 pound hunk of tissue a careful inspection. "It looks fine."

Once again Vanity came through, delivering a "perfect placenta." I could not wait to share this visual with Bob—maybe over breakfast?

My tired wife stood. "Can you take care of it?"

More glamor. "Happy to." Like an alien bloody mass, the afterbirth sat in the bottom of a manure bucket. In the morning, I would dump it in the woods where unspeakable events would occur and it would disappear in two days.

In the meantime, the baby nursed and the mare ate, drank, and nuzzled the colt. That baby would grow to 18 hands and weigh 2,200 pounds.

As we watched Vanity and her baby, my wife smiled and sighed. "Well, that was easy."

Happy horsin'.

CHAPTER 11

Barns, Bad Weather & Stall Mats

Hello, boys. If a house for dogs is called a dog house, what do you call a house for horses? A hor—never mind, just call it a barn. Dog houses are cheap since dogs are little. Horses are not little, barns are not cheap.

Our first farm in Ohio, way back in 1997, came with a barn. Twenty years old, it had four stalls, Dutch doors, electricity and water, a 12' x 12' tack room, and an attic for hay storage. That first winter, the unheated tack room equaled the outdoor temperatures. We had turned off the tack room water, but who needs a tack room with no water? Cold and unpleasant, the next year we got a small ceramic heater that allowed for liquid water and an ambient temperature of 40 degrees. Despite the improvements, and with an expanding herd of horses, the old barn did not do the job; too cold, rickety-tickety, and too small.

We solved the problem by spending a fortune. We hired the Amish horse-barn-and-indoor-arena builders to build. Unlike the 1980's movie *Witness*, where 100 men arrived and completed the job in one day, then ate fried chicken from long tables covered with blue-checkered tablecloths, ours was a small crew that worked daily for three months and ate in their trucks. In the end, we got a huge tack room with heating and AC, eight stalls, a nice sized apartment, hay storage in the attic, and a 14,000 square foot indoor riding arena. It was hands-down better than our house, recently remodeled by a contractor we never found after he got 90% of our money.

The Ohio barn was a solid, four-season facility. For our last years in Ohio, it served us perfectly. When we moved to Florida, we discovered one and a half season barns. Like a screen door on an aquarium and permeable to everything, a bad idea. These "barns" had dirt floors, a roof, light aluminum bars halfway up each wall, and were open to the outside. I get that it is hot in Florida but sometimes it is cold, and many times it is windy and raining. I like real barns that you can close up when needed. If it's too hot, put a fan in the upper corner of each stall. They work.

Barns and Florida must also be considered in the context of hurricanes—we enjoyed three during our six-year hitch in the tropics—and the issues surrounding horses.

I remember the first and worst hurricane.

Anticipating the storm, my wife shook her head. "Do we keep them in stalls or leave them out? I'd hate for them to be in a building that blows over."

I shared her angst, but more for us and our dog Yogi. Our house seemed flimsy as the wind rattled the windows.

I scratched my chin. "Those stalls are like card houses and may blow over. If they stay out, they can at least dodge the stall walls and other stuff that might be flying around. They might find their own version of safe cover if we leave them out."

"I read on the internet we should spray paint our phone number on them in case they get away."

I had neither the spray paint nor the desire to spray, thinking it was a clever if not crazy idea.

I took her nervous hand. "No. Every time they escape a paddock, they hang right at the gate anyway. This is where they get fed, they won't leave."

In the end, we left them out. Unlike us humans, they came through unscathed. Although we were uninjured and our house survived, our electricity did not. It stayed off for five days. After 20 inches of rain in two days, the sun came out and turned northern Florida into a steamy, smothery blast furnace. The house was a miserable sauna, we stuck to everything. Our water came from a well with an electric pump. No flushing. No showering. We had a pool which offered a dodgy water source for both people and horses. By the third day, it was 95 in the house and so humid I wondered if the drywall would liquify and our pictures slide down to the floor.

The next street north of us and all the way to Georgia, had electricity. It was dark from our place south for 350 miles to Miami. We found out later that our county was the northern-most outpost of the south Florida power grid.

On day four, I acted. "Enough, we are going to a hotel."

We got a suite, dog and all, and nearly cried with joy.

My happy wife smiled. "This is wonderful."

Already with the receiver to my ear, I was dialing. "I am ordering us a generator."

We had a two-day mini-vacation then went back home for clean-up. My generator came ten days later. I suffered endless ridicule from natives who said I was nuts. They looked at the dumb Yankee. "The last big one was in 1964, this was a real exception."

The second hurricane came within a month. With a smile, I ran my little generator, powering all our appliances and a bevy of house fans for three days. The milk and frozen food survived. If you have a farm anywhere, buy a generator. We don't get much from hurricanes in Aiken but did have an ice storm that shut things down for a week, generating more generator-smiles.

We never got used to the open stalls of Florida, so when we came to Aiken, we built a real barn. We also saw many shed barns that have stalls open to the elements, but we wanted to go back to an enclosed building with tack room, wash stall, etcetera. Perhaps hotter in the summer, but when we open the Dutch doors, it stays cooler than the outside temperature.

One feature of our barn we like is the overhang at one end for parking the tractor. This keeps it out of the elements but still offers easy access. The plans called for the overhang to be at the north end of the barn. Construction was underway while we were still in Florida, but we came up on a regular basis to enjoy the progress.

The week before one visit, they had poured the concrete slab for the barn. After arriving on Saturday morning, we walked around the site. At the south end, she pointed. "What are these holes for?"

"Hmm, I'm not sure."

On the north side, there were no holes. Her brow furrowed, she looked at me. "Where are the holes for the overhang posts?"

"I don't know."

"I think they got it backwards. The overhang is at the wrong end."

We practically raced over to the barn builder's office, still open that morning.

As we stood in his office, she nudged me to speak. "Well Hudson, the barn's coming along."

"Yep, real good, too."

"So Hud, can we take a peek at the plans?"

The three of us hunched over the blueprints.

My wife wasted no time. "Where's the overhang?"

"Right here," he said, pointing at the south end.

I nodded. "Ah, Hud, it was supposed to be at the north end."

"Yeah? Let's see. Is that where you want it?"

"Yes."

"No problem, we can move it. The slab's the same. How's everything else?"

So elated about our rescued overhang we could not come up with anything else. To this day, we thank our lucky stars we made the trip that weekend.

When building a barn, there are endless controversies over lights, stall doors, Dutch doors, door latches, and of critical relevance to all barns and the bane of all horse husbands, stall mats.

The floors of your stalls will be the ground. A good builder will pack it down, and lay the stall mats for you. If he does not pack the ground and puts down the mats anyway, he is not a good builder. Your stall floors beneath the mats will soon be lumpy, your wife grumpy. Her grumpiness is nothing next to yours when you have to move the heavy, grungy mats, then somehow try to smooth and pack down the floor. Call somebody, this job is too big for you.

Stall mats also serve another purpose, and this you may also want to out-source. To soften the walk down the middle aisle of your barn, your wife will want you to put down a long row of the mats. They are like carpet for a horse, thus softer than concrete. The mats will also protect the cement floor from chipping, a result of shoed hooves. You do not want to have to re-do the concrete slab in five years due to heavy horse traffic.

The issue is buying, transporting, and laying down the mats. They are 4 x 6 feet, ¾ inch thick, and weigh 100 pounds. Their single asset is that they are made of recycled rubber and are thus "green." Otherwise, I hate them more than obnoxious horses. There is nothing to grab except the edges, and unless you are a giant, I can guarantee you will have no strength to drag the damn things with your arms spread from edge to edge. And no, they do not bend, roll, nor fold. They are flat and heavy. We needed ten mats to cover the required distance in our central aisle. That is 1,000 pounds of rubber. It took me all day to get them off the truck and into place. I swore "Never again!" but a year later they were dirty and had to be dragged out so I could power wash the floor. On second thought, just re-do the concrete in five years.

It may be that I have convinced you to keep your horses at that public facility—let them worry about the stall mats. On the other hand, if you plan to go the barn route, build a real barn, get a generator, and get the hell out of Florida.

Happy horsin'.

CHAPTER 12

Farminomics

Hello, boys. Let's talk dollars and sense. With horses, there is plenty of the former, and a staggering scarcity of the latter. In short, horses are expensive. But how expensive?

To address the question, let's compare dogs and horses. We have a little dog named Yogi. When he weighed ten pounds, he was worth 100 dollars a pound (do not ask why we paid that much). At 20 pounds, he is now worth 50 dollars a pound. No matter, we still love little Yogi, despite his decline in net worth.

Yogi costs us about $240 a year. Forty dollars for two 20 pound bags of dog food annually. Throw in a $12 bag of pumpkin-squash-all-natural-good-for-his-bowels treats, an annual $120 vet visit to keep him tuned, and let's not forget the daily glucosamine for good joint health at $24 per year, and big anti-flea and tick pills that he will gobble with cheese, at $44 per year. We include the cheese at no charge since we eat it too.

The above ignores the occasional emergency, like the time Yogi got into my sister-in-law's purse and ate three chocolate Hershey bars. Off to the emergency room we went, for a tidy stomach pumping for $350. Yogi seemed unfazed by the experience, although he was sedated and slept for two days afterward. I was privy to being shown the product of the pumping which was the same color as both his food and his stool, raising unrealistic questions in my mind about a novel nutritional recycling program, but at only $40 a year for food, I decided to let it go.

To stay on point, let's ignore the emergency and stick with the monthly cost for the 20 pound dog, around $20. The question that has nagged me for years is whether the economics are consistent on a "by weight" basis. Testing this question, we find that for a horse that is 100 times heavier than Yogi, at 2,000 pounds, we would predict about $2,000 per month or $24,000 per year. Sound steep? If it does, then you are (blissfully (?)) uninformed about where your money goes, since it's a pretty good number. I will avoid asking who manages the money at your house.

So what contributes to the twenty-four grand? Our horses are at our place, but if boarded out, would cost around $500 per month or $6,000 annually (for one horse). Note, we are already twenty-five percent of the way toward the total. Keeping to the one-horse model, there is another six grand in several items. Unproven dietary supplements are crucial and cost another $2,000 per year. Not included is the monthly Metamucil for good bowel health, and Kirkland-brand tums as a cheap horse treat, both from Costco and inexpensive. Then there are farrier visits to trim those toenails (eight times a year totaling $1,600), the equine dentist four times a year (filing down those sharp molars, under sedation, in the cross ties, for another $1,200) and miscellaneous unproven visits from the horse chiropractor, the acupuncturist, and a single visit from a psychic (even my wife thought that was a little weird). Weird or not, these recreational assessments amount to another $1,200 annually for a total of six grand. So, in keeping a horse eating, pooping, and moving around, we spend about $12,000 per year. With more horses (which we have), it is more expensive, but there may be bulk discounts, etc., all beyond the scope of this simple analysis. Please note, if you board your horses somewhere, these are the costs, and you are done. But we spoke of $24,000. So where's the other twelve grand? Well, one place. Your farm.

Like humans, animals require housing and maintenance. Yogi lives with us rent-free. Even if he had a little summer doghouse in the back yard, the cost would be zilch. He also requires 1,000 square feet for walking, peeing, and pooping, the horses need much more. I will confess that Yogi's little outdoor latrine is part of our larger yard requiring a 60 inch, zero-turn diesel mower ($10,000), so his costs are not exactly zilch, but like the cheese, it is included in the deal. Anyway, doing the math, Yogi's one thousand square feet of yard is .02 acres. Following the by-weight analogy, each horse needs about one hundred times this area, or two acres. Here lies your other twelve grand: land, the necessary accouterments for sustainability, and shelter.

To keep things nice for the babies, you must invest (poor term, I meant "buy," for there will be no return on this investment) in a barn ($130,000), a tractor with a 3 point hitch ($20,000) for running a bush hog ($8,000), broadcast fertilizer ($500), and sprayer ($1,500). You need a building to store all this equipment or you will replace it every three years as a result of exposure. Hence an equipment shed ($100,000) is indicated. You need a spreader ($1,000) since your little equine manure factories will each make a bucket a day. If you do not spread, you will die of some dreaded horse-poop bug infection, or be forced to move from the deafening buzz of flies and the eye-watering burn of a stinky "manure pile" in the back corner of your property. Yuck. Tap your retirement account, buy a spreader, and spread the poop.

Corralling animals is necessary. Yogi has a leash, the horses have fence, lots of fence. Fifty grand for fence and this ignores your time (valued less than Yogi's) at fixing boards popped off by horses with itchy butts.

So, back to the math. The total for horse housing and maintenance is around $300,000. Stretch it over 20 years (if you are lucky), and you get $15,000 per year. Add it to the above twelve grand, and we get $27,000 per year. Hmm. That sure worked out. By the way, I suspect this is similar to how the government presents its budget, a little fuzzy around the edges.

I have ignored the drag(s) to keep the arena groomed, the power washer to keep the barn sparkly, the generator to keep the lights on when they go off, pasture maintenance (tons of lime, fertilizer, and winter rye), as well as all amenities to make the barn and tack room a nicer place (washer, drier, dehumidifier, window AC, and 4,000 plastic storage bins that are full of god-knows-what all).

The last financial black hole is animal travel. Yogi jumps into the back seat when being transported, whereas the horses require a bit more; a gooseneck, two-bay trailer ($25,000), pulled by a Ford F-150 ($25,000 in 2004, delivering a stellar nine mpg). Much of the above may be classified as miscellaneous expenses, so they do not count toward actual horse costs. This selective accounting is how your horse wife can move expenses from "horses" to "other."

Now you know the meaning of "ignorance is bliss," and I apologize for the depressing audit. So what's a poor horse husband to do? Well, if you keep the horses, forget about retirement. If you cannot get rid of them, at least send them to a public barn, sell the farm, buy a condo, and get a dog.

Happy horsin'.

CHAPTER 13

Of Golf Carts & Gators

Hello, boys. Face it, you're married to a horse girl. You think you're in charge. But, in fact, you are not. Do not confuse possession of the TV remote with domestic control. Or, offering a more positive spin, the remote represents your only micro sliver of power. Let's examine why.

Consider a conceptual model. Think of a bicycle wheel: an outer rim, with spokes leading to a central hub. The hub, of course, is the barn that houses your wife's babies. On top of the barn sits a golden throne, on which perches your wife, riding crop raised to heaven in one hand, a horse treat clutched in the other. Adorned with a horse-themed tee shirt and skin-tight riding pants, you can at least admire the view when she gets up and walks away.

Anyway, you are relegated to the rim, moving around and around in an infinite circle, pouring substrate into the spokes that feed and support the palatial hub. What are these spokes? There are at least eight, each of which is named for an element critical to every farm: manure, farriers, veterinarians, fence, fields, feed, barn, and vehicles. Like the ancient roads of Italy leading to, and in support of, the emperor in Rome, your spokes lead to and support your local empress. And like the ancients, you are but a peasant, circling around your little rim in crummy sandals and an itchy burlap tunic. However, do not despair, our ancient masculine ancestors found pleasure in their ox carts. Likewise, we modern horse husbands are enamored of our wheels.

All guys like vehicles. They offer an illusion of power and save us the trouble of walking. On the farm, that precludes wasting time and offers you more opportunities to play golf, or fiddle with the remote. Let's examine a representative spectrum of farm vehicles. This may include trucks, tractors, and two potential "G" words, golf carts and Gators, the real subject of this discussion.

These vehicles are smaller than trucks and tractors and are intended to help zip around the property. They facilitate your performance of an infinite number of small jobs that constitute several spokes of the above conceptual prison. Golf carts and Gators share functional similarities but have radically different personalities.

Using a Hollywood analogy, one is Arnold Schwarzenegger, the other is Woody Allen. You can probably guess which is who. Gators (diesel) are studs (Arnold), golf carts (electric) are duds (Woody).

I am a proud owner of a dud. In fact, we are in our twenty-first year of dud ownership, having inherited the first of three in 1997. The second lasted 16 years, and the third is now one month old. Eight years ago, number two was getting sluggish, so, for the very first time, I had somebody look at it.

The guy proclaimed that the batteries were dead, and "when were they last changed?"

"Why, never," I told him. I guess it is hard to shock an electric golf cart mechanic, but he was so incredulous he had to sit down. As he stared at me, slack-jawed and bewildered, I told him we plugged it in when it got sluggish, and I filled the batteries with water now and then, but otherwise, that was it. I did mention putting air in the tires if it seemed to slow down. Gators go faster too, if the tires are not flat.

"Well sir, this is the longest time I have ever seen a golf cart's batteries last. We will put in a new set. I will not tell you how to care for them. Whatever I tell you will not be as good as whatever the hell you do."

This concluded my first encounter with a golf cart mechanic and suggested to me that one could consider electric golf carts low maintenance, and cheap to operate. Although I must confess that I have a $150 air compressor to help keep the tires inflated, but its cost can be spread across all the other tires on the farm (between cars, mowers, spreader, horse trailer, and several hand carts, this totals 30).

My golf cart is Gator-oid, in that instead of a platform for golf clubs behind the front seat, it has a small utility bed with a tailgate and a dump function. Unlike a Gator, my golf cart is quiet, spews no blue smoke, and does not stink, unless there are muck buckets full of manure in the utility bed. With a diesel Gator, you would either welcome or not notice, the manure smell, depending on your particular proclivity.

The electric golf cart is the embodiment of Zen on the farm. It is quiet and unobtrusive, offering a demeanor that allows one to enjoy whatever journey is needed between tasks. Ahhh, I feel myself relaxing as I write this. Contrast this with a noisy, sputtering green monster, ejecting fumes and stink across the paddocks, and scaring the dickens out of the horses. The latter constitutes a significant risk to your marriage, and no doubt leads to the recurrent argument over why you insisted on the damn Gator. Or maybe not. I am just speculating.

One horse lady commented to my wife that their Gator was in the shop more than on the farm. "In the shop" does not mean you dropped off a lamp with a faulty cord. No, it means you had to call John Deere and arrange to have the thing picked up (now sitting lifeless in a distant paddock) and somebody has to be home to meet the Deere boys. This somebody is often your horse wife, who invariably has plans that are being interrupted because you insisted on buying that stupid Gator. Again, pure speculation.

Another advantage of the electric golf cart is that I get to drive a golf cart. I no longer play golf, since my job and the farm occupy all my time, but it keeps my cart-driving skills up to par if I ever play again. Golf aside, I must also mention that Ohio State has lost too many times to Florida, so I am predisposed to disliking Gators.

So, whether Gator or golf cart, keep smiling and enjoy your life on the rim.

Happy horsin'.

CHAPTER 14

The Fletcher in the Rye

Hello, boys. As I write this, our horse Fletcher is grazing in the winter rye, reminding me of the learning curve for pasture management. If you don't have a farm, skip this chapter as it will deter you from buying one. And be clear, this will have no effect on your wife—she will still want a farm whether she reads this or not. Since sooner or later you will end up with a farm, you might as well read on for a glimpse of your future.

As you lay the groundwork for your farm, you and your wife will agree that the first question is how much acreage will you need? The obvious answer is also a question; how many horses will you have? From here, you and your wife will disagree. The discussion will go something like this:

"Mary, just how many horses will we have?"

"Why I don't know yet, but I know it will be cheaper if we have our own place for Wally and Rugger. Besides, at the public barn they don't get turned out enough, the help skims on the feed, the hay is not very good, and the stalls are never clean."

You scratch your head at her use of the term "cheaper." At the time of this discussion, you will not have read the chapter in this book on Equinomics, where we showed how you *never* lose money on horses. Curiously, it looks like Mary has.

You forge ahead. "Can you take a guess?"

"At least two. Maybe four or five."

You will need to plan for six. Odd numbers of horses do not work. It's pairs or nothing. Single horses get lonely and are unhappy. Three horses mean two will gang up on one, and the odd-man-out will be unhappy. More than three horses together in a paddock is a herd and requires more acreage than the prairies of western Kansas.

You also need to know the optimal ratio of horses to acres. In Aiken and most of the south, two acres per horse is the consensus. But with supplemental hay, you can get by with fewer acres. You could also have fewer horses, but we both know that is a non-starter.

Once you have your acres, fence, and other "necessities" (see Chapter 12, Farminomics), you must consider the grass in your paddocks as a crop and care for it. Otherwise, the pastures become weed-infested and grow nothing the horses will eat. This will force you to buy more hay, suggesting an increase in costs. Then again, maybe not. Taking care of pastures is expensive and hard work. If you have somebody else do the labor (a good idea), it's more expensive, but you will be free to watch TV or play golf, assuming there is any money left.

Think of your paddocks as a big lawn, and your lawn needs fertilizer. I follow a fertilizing schedule necessitating regular treatments. It is also suggested that pre-emergent weed killer be placed every October and February.

I can sense your rising desire to not have a farm, but relax,

I do not put pre-emergent down inside the rails. With healthy grass in the paddocks, weeds are uncommon. This also brings up the unexpected question of how you define a "weed." My wife helped me understand that a "weed" is anything a horse will not eat. This very broad definition excludes horse edibles like dandelions, blackberry plants, and just about everything else you thought was a yard weed. This illustrates an asset to having a horse in a field—an 1,800 pound weed-eater. Goats might serve the same purpose, but I draw the line at horses. We are and will remain, goat-less.

We have about ten acres inside the fences that need June lime and fertilizer. I do it, triggering the need for equipment. Our tractor has a three-point hitch that drives a wonderful broadcast spreader holding 300 pounds of dry product. The spreader slings about ten feet on either side of the tractor, so I can cover a lot of ground with a single lap. It's by far my favorite piece of equipment since it is so efficient. The downside: It goes through 300 pounds of the material ten times faster than it takes to fill it.

With what do I fill it, you ask? Try 50-pound bags of fertilizer and lime. Last year the dosing guidelines dictated 80 bags of lime and 40 bags of fertilizer, for a total of 6,000 pounds, every pound hoisted by the author. It costs less than $2,000. The lime gets laid down two weeks before the fertilizer. After both are down, you pray for rain.

All the product makes better grass for grazing. We have Bermuda grass in our paddocks. It's green until the first cold snap. Then it retires, yielding acres of brown. In late spring, when the ground temperature is above 50 degrees, we green-up. When we first moved to Aiken, our horses fiddled with brown Bermuda but did not seem very interested, necessitating lots of hay. I was amazed at how some people were able to keep their Bermuda so green during the winter. The golf courses too, for that matter.

That is how I discovered winter ryegrass.

Winter rye is what keeps the South green year around. The good news is that it's green, makes the paddocks look like Ireland, and gives the horses something to do besides stand at the gate waiting for their evening grain allocation. The bad news is that it requires another trip to the seed store for both rye seed and more fertilizer and, for our place, a cash outlay of about $1,600. Ever eat rye bread with those little seeds? Our rye seeds look just like that. I will leave what fertilizer looks like to your imagination.

The rye is laid down in late September or October, followed by more prayers for rain. This makes paddock management a religious experience. No rain, no grain. That happened one year. We got no rain until March, at which time the rye popped up. Three weeks later it was 90 degrees and it all died from the heat. In the last few years, we have had substantial autumn rains and mild temperatures, making our paddocks look like Augusta National. Our horses like the rye and it reduces their need for supplemental hay. But, as your wife will tell you, rye alone is not enough. They still need to be fed all the other "stuff."

With good rye, you also get good conversation.

Your wife points at the pasture. "The rye came in great, but I think Wally is getting fat."

You nod, with no idea how you can tell a fat horse. "Oh."

She smiles. "I am so happy. I can tell they are no longer bored and are enjoying their days."

You had always considered the steady production of manure a surrogate for horse enjoyment, but keep this to yourself. "Yeah, I imagine you are right."

As the rye goes into the horse, manure comes out. When it comes out in a stall, it gets removed, but what do you do with piles in the paddocks? Nothing, you say. It's nature, it will break down.

How *does* manure "break down?" Microorganisms and turd beetles. Both eat the stuff and turn it into brown dust after about a week, which is good.

Unfortunately, during that week, the fresh poop smothers the grass beneath, which dies. This is bad. Worse yet, fresh manure offers a nice home for intestinal parasites to live and thrive. This might explain why horses don't graze within about a five-foot radius of a pile. The surface area thus lost to grazing calculates to about 75 square feet per pile. An acre has 43,000 square feet, meaning it will take 500 piles to destroy one acre.

"It's only 500," you muse.

Only, you think? Let's run the numbers. One horse drops about seven loads a day or 50 per week. We have two horses in said paddock, this ups the total to 100 piles per week. If we do not do something, we'll run out of an acre of graze-able grass in about a month. *Only* a month.

Unless you own all of Aiken County, you need a plan for the poop.

Manure is discussed elsewhere in this book, but for now,

consider this. Smaller paddocks can and should be picked each day. This preserves the limited graze-able land. Over time, horses will eat in areas that have been picked. We also have a six-acre tract and drag the piles each week. Breaking them up is as effective as scooping them; the horses will graze areas with broken up piles and the grass below lives.

It may irritate the turd beetles, but you can't make everybody happy.

Say each manure pile weighs seven pounds. For our two horses residing in the six-acre tract, that is 700 pounds of poop per week or 35,000 pounds of potential fertilizer per year. Frankly, dragging the six acres each week is a hell of a lot easier than spreading 35,000 pounds of bag-fertilizer.

That public barn and your wimpy little suburban house are looking better by the minute, eh?

Perhaps like the protagonist behind the namesake of this essay, I've generated not teenage, but *pasture* angst. But to be clear, there is no manure in these words, pasture care is serious business, for your horses, your wife, your marriage, and for better or worse, the fertilizer store.

Happy horsin'.

CHAPTER 15

Bugs

Hello, boys. Mix horses with grass and you get manure. Once you get manure, you get bugs. To name a few, flies, gnats, and turd beetles, although the latter are good guys. But overall, unless you are a cattle egret, bugs are an unpleasant problem. Bugs also include armyworms and, my favorite, parasitic wasps. Similar to turd beetles, they are good to have around.

We went to Charleston one weekend. My wife checked her email. "We might have armyworms."

Ripped from the television and my fantasy of the next great meal, I looked at her. "We might? And what's an armyworm?" I offered my loopiest grin. "Like, from the Citadel?"

No response. "There's a notice from the homeowners association that several people's paddocks have been eaten by armyworms. They say they can devour an acre an hour."

"*Horses* can't devour an acre an hour, and they are much bigger."

"I think we should go home. I did notice a few worms on the cement in front of the barn. I hope they weren't armyworms."

"Oh, will you relax? We leave tomorrow anyway."

We stuck it out and left the next day, returning to an army-worm farm. Parts of our green paddocks were brown, despite good rain. Not reminding me that she wanted to leave a day earlier remains a true gesture of love, a kindness I will never forget.

Squatting in front of the barn, she pointed. "Look at 'em all. Is the grass moving?"

I squinted. "Yes." It looked like a tumultuous ocean. Well, maybe not that bad, but on closer examination, worms could be seen twisting through the Bermuda. "Do armyworms make army moths? And what do *they* eat?"

This brought a whole new level of angst.

She turned toward the house. "I'm going in and Google."

Within twenty minutes she knew the entire life cycle of an armyworm and identified an effective liquid pesticide. By the twenty-second minute I was on my way to Lowes, and in an hour was back home hooking our beam sprayer to the tractor.

The implement, purchased for a cheap price from TSC, showed us that we got what we paid for. First, hooking the thing up requires popping the hood of the tractor and tapping the battery to run the sprayer's electric pump. This is annoying. Then, and after running cables from the tractor battery to the sprayer motor, the sprayer apparatus is attached to the three-point hitch at the back of the tractor. Next, things broke. Over the first year, the pump had to be replaced, the filters grew clogged, and the plastic stopcocks started leaking. No mechanical genius, I managed to make the needed repairs, allowing the thing to keep working. In this time of armyworms, and cheap as it was, it was ready for the challenge.

The sprayer beam is eight or ten feet in width and allows

for wide coverage with each lap in the paddock, making the actual spraying efficient. This assumes the sprayer is attached to the tractor correctly.

As the name implies, a three-point hitch hooks the sprayer to the tractor at three points. On the day of the spray, I got two out of three, which is not bad if you are throwing strikes, but not good enough if you want the sprayer to remain attached to the tractor. I pulled into the first paddock and heard a terrible noise, followed by increased resistance in pulling. Checking the sprayer, it had come off the unsecured third point and was dragging on the ground. The sprayer tank contained 30 gallons of liquid anti-armyworm, and at 8.34 pounds per gallon, it weighed 250 pounds. Raising the load with the two remaining points got the lopsided sprayer high enough for me to re-hook the apparatus and insert the crucial cotter pin that I had forgotten. After a sweaty 45 minutes, the spraying began. Nervous, I feared for the half-acre that had been consumed during this critical delay. But in the end, we won. The worms were defeated, the Bermuda and my marriage, secure.

Other bugs include the ubiquitous housefly. Synonymous with manure, houseflies act as a hygienic barometer; the more you have, the grungier your farm. To deal with flies, you can capture or prevent. In Ohio, capturing with "fly strips" and "fly traps" was popular. But, these reservoirs eventually fill up and stink with the rotting corpses of flies dumb enough to get caught. I had a passing thought about whether smart flies, the uncaught, had better insect hygiene and did not stink. You might appreciate that I should stick with writing and not thinking.

We prefer prevention. Meticulous attention to manure—scooping and spreading (or removing) on a regular basis—decreases housing opportunities for the flies. We also employ parasitic wasps, including the awesomely named *Muscidifurax raptor*. At 1.5 millimeters in length, we could fit over 100 of the things on one line of this page. These tiny wasps lay their eggs in the pupa of the flies, the phase between a maggot and a fly, where baby raptors feast on the sleeping future pest, making more raptors and fewer flies. I could see a little raptor tee-shirt, "Got maggots?"

Every year we buy small bags of the wasps, scattering them in our manure spreader and across the fields. I think they work. It seems like we have fewer flies than before.

Less good are Aiken gnats. No matter the time of year, if it is sunny and above freezing, they can be found buzzing over a fresh pile of poop or exploring horse ears. Like the movie, *With Six You Get Egg Rolls*, on the farm, it's *With Gnats You Get Fly Masks*. A fly mask is a piece of cloth screen with a Velcro strap, that covers eyes, ears, or body. In Ohio, our fly masks were eyes only. The lack of ear sheaths make the orientation of eyes-only masks nebulous; I tended to put them on upside down, and thus protected the jaws from flies.

We discovered the eared fly-mask in Florida. And good thing we did since like everything else that buzzes down there, the flies and the gnats were horrendous. Sheathing the ears stopped the constant head shaking and associated weight loss. True or not, there was the impression that our horses burned a lot of calories shaking to beat the bugs.

I have no experience with total-body fly masks, on the

internet referred to as fly sheets. These are gigantic sheets of screen worn by the horse. What a great idea—wrap your horse in a blanket when it is 90 degrees and 100 percent humidity. Bugs will not be a problem, the horse will die from heat exhaustion and dehydration. Better yet, buy one off the internet that is impregnated with insecticide. You can add cancer to the above causes of death. These comments also underscore how easy it is to offer a stream of useless opinions when you are ignorant of a topic. If you are a fly-sheeter, I am sure you recognize sheet when you read it.

Bifenthrin is an insecticide. The year after the armyworms, we put it down on the areas of our property that were outside the fences. As that summer wound down, my wife and I walked around our property. I opened my arms to the lovely green pastures. "Well, no more armyworms, and you know, it seemed like the dog had fewer fleas and ticks this year." I felt happy.

She paused to examine some flowers in the mulch bed. "Where are all the bees?"

My elation faded as we looked around. She was right, there were no honey bees.

Once in the house, she clicked away at her keyboard. "That stuff you put down kills bees." I felt terrible since bees are harmless and good for our plants.

Close to tears, I shook my head. "I didn't know."

"And you were going to put it down in the fields. I bet it would wipe out the turd beetles too."

Between the mass murder of the bees and my potential assault on the unsuspecting turd beetles, I almost went to the sheriff and turned myself in. But in the end, we just put the kibosh on insecticiding the fields, leaving me with twenty-five bags of bifenthrin glowing like uranium in the corner of the shed. At least that area is bug-free.

The happy ending is that we no longer use insecticide, relying on fly-masks for horses, and dog baths for little Yogi.

Six months after the loss of the bees, my wife called me to her computer. "I found a honey bee class you should take. You have been whining about the bees long enough. Take the class, get a hive."

"What about bees and horses?" If one got stung, I was a goner.

She gazed at her screen. "Bees like horse sweat but they like flowers more. We have 20 acres, find a spot away from the horses."

I did. We now have a hive. No honey yet, but a hive. And our flowers look better. I bought the hive, suit, gloves, and a 4,000-bee starter pack, with queen, all for the price of one month of horse feed. Cost-effective and green. Like a Prius.

Let's close with turd beetles. For cocktail parties, use the terms dung beetles. Also known as rollers. They roll dung, they may roll rocks. Of course, this leads to "the rock and roll of the beetles." That's right up there with Ringo's boots (see chapter 2, "Fashion Statements"). According to the internet, dung beetles are among the strongest of insects, some pulling over 1,000 times their weight. Another, "are you kidding?", fact—they navigate by the Milky Way. Love to know who the poor grad student was who got *that* assignment.

I have no data on daily turd volume processed, but I do

know that a pile left alone in the field during the summer, and with clear nights for navigation, is reduced to brown dust in less than five days. Ergo, turd beetles are good and they will never see bifenthrin.

So, that's bugs. And the next time you take a midnight stroll with your wife, remember this: navigate by the stars and don't be a turd.

Happy horsin'.

Epilogue

And so it goes. At this writing, we have four horses who are aging. Of the four, three are old enough to be nursing home material, but one can still carry my wife on the horse trails, so he does. And like her, he still enjoys it. The youngest has great potential, but a personality disorder that makes him obnoxious, and to me, annoying. But he is a horse, which is the single requisite attribute for my wife to love him, so he stays.

Through the wry prism of a horse husband, I have used this book to explore many facets of the horse world. Several areas remain untapped, including trainers, horse shows, farriers, and barn help, to name a few. Perhaps I will look at these and other topics someday.

Reflecting on my perception of the horse world as I prepared these chapters, I came to realize that horses are good to have around. Let's be clear, they are not cheap, but they do offer some interesting characteristics. We have one that will come when I call his name. This makes me happy. Another will drink a gallon from the water trough, and then offer to share it, dribbling over everything with his tongue between his teeth, and sticking out of his mouth a short inch. This gets me wet but is entertaining. And we do not have biters, meeting my minimal litmus test for citizenship. These qualities do not begin to scratch the surface of what a horsewoman sees in horses, but they are enough for me and maybe for you.

So, as you follow your wife into the paddocks of the future, get on board. You will enjoy making her happy, driving the tractor, and fussing with the big guys. They will bond with you through feeding, no matter your skill set. But the day may come when she will ask you to ride with her. Do it and get a glimpse of the joy horses can bring, but be sure to check the cinch.

Happy horsin'.

Acknowledgments

I want to thank my colleagues of the Aiken Chapter of the South Carolina Writers Association for their guidance and unvarnished critiques of the manuscript. So much I thought was funny, just wasn't; so much detail I thought was important, just wasn't. As you might guess, they have not had a chance to edit these lines. Damn the torpedoes, on this one I will go it alone.

A special thanks to Aiken author and dedicated horsewoman Ruth Kipnis for her comments on the content and generous guidance on what to do with this book. Ruth, my appreciation for your kindness to a perfect stranger cannot be overstated.

In closing, I want to offer my deepest thanks to my colleague from the Aiken Chapter, Amy Blunt, whose sharp eye and knowledge of horses brought needed quality to the work. And she never once said that after reading my stuff that her head was Aiken.